TREVOR GRAHAM is an acclaimed Australian documentary producer and director. He is the director of Yarra Bank Films Pty Ltd, a Sydney-based company that was founded in 1983. Trevor's documentaries have been screened and broadcast around the world. He has produced and directed films for Channel 4 (Britain), the BBC, PBS (America), ABC TV and SBS. His films have won numerous national and international film and television awards and nominations, most recently *Mabo – Life of an Island Man*, winner of the Australian Film Institute's Award for Best Documentary 1997. *Mabo* was also awarded the NSW Premier's Literary Award for Best Screenplay in 1997 and a NSW Premier's History Award.

In 1995 Trevor's film *Aeroplane Dance* won a Silver Hugo at the Chicago International Film Festival and the Royal Anthropological Society's prestigious Basil Wright Prize in 1997. Among his credits are, *Red Matildas*, *Painting the Town* (winner AFI Award Best Documentary1987), *Land Bilong Islanders*, *Aeroplane Dance*, *Dancing In the Moonlight*, *Paper Trail*, *Sugar Slaves*, *Punchlines* and *Mystique of the Pearl*.

Trevor is currently the Head of Documentary at the Australian Film Television and Radio School in Sydney. He is also co-directing a CD ROM and web-site production on the Mabo case for Film Australia.

Mabo
Life of an Island Man

Original Screenplay by
Trevor Graham

Currency Press • Sydney

First published 1999 by
Currency Press Ltd,
PO Box 2287, Strawberry Hills,
NSW 2012, Australia
www.currency.com.au
currency@magna.com.au

NATIONAL LIBRARY OF AUSTRALIA CIP DATA
Graham, Trevor
    Mabo: life of an island man.
    ISBN 0 86819 580 4.
    1. Motion picture plays. I. Title.
791.437

Printed by.Southwood Press, Marrickville, NSW
Cover design by Libby Blainey

PHOTOGRAPHIC ACKNOWLEDGMENTS: Location shots used within the text were taken by Trevor Graham. Shots taken during the launch at the State Theatre, Sydney, were taken by Corrie Ancone. Family shots are courtesy of the Mabo family.

Contents

Acknowledgments

With most film projects that come to fruition there are so many people to thank who have contributed their skills, their ideas, their talent and their passions. But *Mabo – Life of an Island Man* was made over a period of eight years, so I figure the normal thank-yous should be multiplied at least by a factor of eight.

The documentary would never have been made without the commitment of Eddie Mabo, his wife Bonita and their children. Eddie Jnr, Gail, Bethel, Celuia, Mal, Jessie, Malita, Mario, Ezra and Wannee all spent time with me at some stage talking about their dad. There are thirty-four grandchildren who were also exposed to the hazards of filmmaking. I thank them all for their patience, their love and their endurance over those eight years. The Mabos are a wonderful clan and a great advertisement for large extended families.

Sharon Connolly was my partner in crime at Yarra Bank Films in the late nineteen eighties, was there at the beginning, produced *Land Bilong Islanders* and was executive producer on *Mabo* for Film Australia. The films we've made bear her stamp as much as mine. My DoP John Whitteron and sound recordist Bronwyn Murphy also accompanied me on this long saga. We travelled to Murray Island many times and managed to enjoy each other's company despite the rigours of filmmaking and the lugging of tripods and camera boxes up and down the main track of Mer.

My partner of many years Judy Bell befriended the Mabos as much as I did. She spent many an afternoon baby sitting grandchildren, giving us the peace and quiet to get on with filming in the Mabo household. Judy also assisted with the research on *Mabo* and provided me with an endless supply of ethnographic and history books. We travelled to Murray Island together and both felt the enormous power and spirit of Las, the religious centre of Mer where Eddie Mabo grew up. I am indebted to Judy for her love, support and the consideration she gave me throughout those years.

The producer and editor of *Mabo*, Denise Haslem, shares the success of the film as much as I do. It was Denise who encouraged me more than anyone else to personalise the Mabo story. She always said, 'Eddie's a hero but the film has to move people'. Denise was also my script editor when I was writing and we spent many an afternoon in our office at Film Australia discussing Joseph Campbell's idea of the 'hero's journey'. We also talked about the impossibility of 'truth' in documentary. There are 'truths' but not 'the truth'. We decided with *Mabo* that 'emotional truth' would be the key to telling a compelling story. I cannot thank Denise enough for her creative input to the script – she is a soul mate.

The *Mabo* script includes short excerpts of sound recordings of Eddie Mabo speaking about his life. These recordings formed the basis of the biography, *Edward Koiki Mabo: His Life and Struggle for Land Rights*. I'm indebted to author Noel Loos and Queensland University Press for permission to include these excerpts in my writing.

I'd like to thank Film Australia for assisting the script development, producing the film and supporting Denise and me through some difficult stages in post-production. Former CEO Bruce Moir gave his seal of approval to the feature-length film we'd created.

Bob Connolly read a draft of this book, made comments and provided thoughtful insights into the methodologies for writing and directing documentary. Peter Giles the Head of Digital Media at the Australian Film Television and Radio School produced the still of Eddie Mabo from the documentary for the front cover.

I'd like also to thank Currency Press and Nick Parsons for choosing to publish the *Mabo* script. It's the first publication of a documentary script in Australia, if not the world. Let's hope there will be many more.

Finally I want to thank the people of Murray Island; the first indigenous people in Australia to have their native title recognised by the Australian legal system. Obviously the films

I've made about Mabo could not have been made without their involvement and endorsement. Sleeping on the beach at Las and fishing with Eddie Mabo and his friend Jack Wailu will be part of my dreaming forever.

Foreword

Rachel Perkins

I remember the excitement at the Melbourne Town Hall as the Australian film industry rose in their hundreds to give a standing ovation at the announcement that *Mabo – Life of an Island Man* had won Best Documentary at the 1997 Australian Film Institute Awards. It was an historic moment as Eddie's wife, Bonita Mabo, and the director, Trevor Graham, took the stage to receive the award. We acknowledged both the power of the film and the extraordinary contribution Eddie Koiki Mabo had made to Australia.

The awards happened at the height of the debate over the Howard Government's amendments to the Native Title legislation. It was obvious that the Government intended to further restrict the rights of indigenous Australians. As numerous actors, directors and producers accepted their awards that night they urged the Government to consider fairly the interests of indigenous people. Even Nicole Kidman wore the colours of the Aboriginal flag pinned to her Armani! As an indigenous filmmaker in the audience that night I was inspired all over again by the possibilities of film.

Mabo – Life of an Island Man is a testament to Eddie's life-long struggle for recognition. In simple terms he sought to be recognised as the heir to his family's land on Mer Island in the Torres Strait. More broadly, however, he struggled to achieve recognition of Torres Strait Islander law, religious belief and sovereignty. His vision is summarised simply at the beginning of the film:

> According to my traditions, those fish, the prawn, whatever in that sea, belongs to my people. And that is important.[1]

When he won the case for his own people, it set an extraordinary precedent for the rest of the country, but it is also important to understand the significance of Mabo's achievement in the context of the Aboriginal and Torres Strait Islander peoples' historical struggle for land rights.

The unfortunate reality is that British settlement in 1788 marked the beginning of an undeclared war against indigenous Australians, for land. It began in the lands of the Gadigal people, territory now known as Sydney, and spread across the country. As the invasion pushed further inland, the indigenous population dropped from an estimated one million people to around three hundred thousand.

Despite this devastation, the fight for land rights continued down the generations. Through violence, strike action, the UN, protests and finally Eddie Koiki Mabo's high-court challenge, we, the indigenous people, finally won on 3 June, 1992.

Suddenly the word 'Mabo' swept across the country and, for indigenous Australians, it embodied the hope that, after over two hundred years, prior ownership would be recognised. In the turbulent months following the High Court finding the country struggled with the reversal of the fundamental principle of it's foundation: *terra nullius*. By Christmas 1993, nearly two years after Eddie Mabo had passed away, at the last sitting of Federal Parliament in the International Year of The World's Indigenous People, Paul Keating's Labor Government voted that native-title legislation become the law of the land.

However, the battle had only just begun. Unlike black law, white law can be changed, and with the landslide victory of the Coalition in 1996, the new Prime Minister John Howard felt he had a mandate to make the Native Title legislation more 'workable', to the detriment of indigenous people.

Howard's introduction of a 'ten-point plan' heralded amendments to the Keating legislation that would erode the implications of the historic Mabo decision.

Today native title is a reality in Australia. Despite legislative restrictions to the Mabo decision, it has had profound effects on this country, particularly upon indigenous communities. As a direct result of the Mabo decision, hundreds of individuals, families and communities have now begun the complex process of documenting their origins through the identification of their lands, language and culture in the same way as Eddie Koiki Mabo did. Throughout the country we are piecing together our 'law' or the cultural information necessary to prove our heritage and connection to the land. Although to date only a few claims have been successful, a widespread process of cultural retrieval has begun.

Aboriginal law is re-emerging across the country and, through the recognition of this law, there has been a fundamental shift in the balance of power toward indigenous people.

I first heard the word 'Mabo' when I was making a film on my father, Charles Perkins, and the Freedom Ride protests he led in 1967. It was my first major film and Trevor was working with me as script editor. He mentioned he'd made a film with a man named 'Eddie Mabo' who was challenging the concept of *terra nullius* through the courts. This was the film *Land Bilong Islanders*, made through Yarra Bank Films, Trevor and Sharon Connolly's company, in 1989. It was made whilst Eddie was still alive and much of the footage in the second film is from this source. At the time I felt the courts were an impossible road and thought little more about the High Court challenge until the findings in 1992. Like everyone else I was swept up in the furore following the unexpected ruling. And like everyone else I had no idea who Eddie Mabo actually was. Five months earlier Eddie had passed away and his family was now only part-way through a mourning period that would culminate in a traditional tombstone opening.

During the process of making *Land Bilong Islanders*, Trevor and his crew had become close to the Mabo family. Without any intention other than to document this major ceremonial event, Bonita, Eddie's wife, invited Trevor up to Townsville again to film the tombstone opening. The subsequent powerful and emotional events that put an end to Eddie's story in 1995 inspired the filmmakers to make another film, *Mabo – Life of an Island Man*.

Trevor Graham assembled the same team in preparation for

the film. Sharon Connolly, the original producer of *Land Bilong Islanders*, had become an Executive Producer at Film Australia. She commissioned the project under the National Interest Program with a broadcast pre-sale to the ABC. Denise Haslem now became both editor and producer, and Trevor again disappeared up to Townsville with cinematographer John Whitteron and sound recordist Bronwyn Murphy.

That was about the last we heard of them until a few months later when Sharon rang to invite me to a screening of the fine cut to give feedback on it's progress. In a dark room at Film Australia, on a clapped-out old editing machine, I watched the film and the extraordinary life of Eddie Mabo unfold. Of course I was completely devastated at the end of the film and wasn't able to give a single editing suggestion as I was convinced they shouldn't change a frame.

At the time Sharon was in the midst of a major battle with the ABC over the length of the film. Apparently the film had been contracted as a one-hour programme with the option to extend to feature length if the ABC agreed it was justified. But they didn't. I recall Sharon saying to me over a smoke in the car park after the screening, 'If they can show a feature doco on Graham Campbell they can bloody show one on Eddie Mabo!' At the time I was the Executive Producer of the Indigenous Programs Unit at the ABC, and I agreed. I advised the ABC Sharon was mounting a serious campaign, which immediately panicked them. It was a major battle of wills but as usual Eddie won and the film went to air at its full and appropriate length.

As Sharon recalls, 'Amidst all the furore at the height of the native-title debate the film offered a window of understanding into the world where the word 'Mabo' came from and gave a focus and an emotional outlet as Australians across the country wept with the Mabo family for the loss of one of Australia's true heroes, Eddie Koiki Mabo'. It was one of the ABC's strongest-rating documentaries.

It is one of the best documentaries I have seen. I am moved by the love and support of the Mabo family and inspired by the deep personal passion and sacrifice that caused such enormous social change. A particular resonance of the film for me is the description of growing up in a home with a father so totally committed to 'The Cause'. The scene I remember most strongly is where Eddie's daughter Gail recalls her father coming home late from work again, crying in despair and frustration, and the next moment his voice rising in an Island song and spreading through the house until everyone else in their beds is singing with him. This is the greatest achievement of the filmmakers: they have taken the word 'Mabo' out of the headlines and introduced us to the man. Through understanding him, we understand the land-rights movement and, just possibly, white Australians will be able to see the crucial necessity for recognition of native title.

Eddie participated in the making of the film in the knowledge that it would educate people about his cause. Eddie Mabo was an educator and a visionary and this book is an expression of his purpose: to spread the word, to inform our thinking and to inspire us to strive for positive social change.

May, 1999

1.   *Mabo – Life of an Island Man*, Trevor Graham, Film Australia.

Director Trevor Graham with Bonita Mabo on Mer, June 1996.

Introduction

Trevor Graham

Mabo is a name that has become synonymous with a legal revolution in Australia. Since 3 June 1992, the date of the now famous High Court judgement, *Mabo* has been a household name emblazoned across our newspapers and television screens. But who was Eddie Mabo and where did he find the heart to fight two Governments in a ten-year legal battle? Was he a visionary, as *The Australian* newspaper claimed in 1993, or just a stirrer and a radical? The answer to that question consumed my working and personal life for almost eight years and climaxed in the feature-length documentary, which I wrote and directed in 1996 and '97, *Mabo – Life of an Island Man.*

I first became interested in the Mabo Case in 1989. I'd travelled to Murray Island to research a film about independence for the Torres Strait Islands. Throughout 1988, the bicentenary year, many Islanders had declared they wanted to secede from Australia. After more than a hundred years of rule by paternalistic Queensland Governments, they wanted their independence. However by the time I reached Murray Island at the beginning of 1989, the independence issue had all but lost momentum. Instead, Murray Islanders were fired up about a legal battle over land ownership being waged by one of their own, Eddie Koiki Mabo.

I returned to Melbourne via Townsville so I could meet with Mabo. Like many Torres Strait Islanders, Koiki had moved to the mainland as a young man in search of work, and he'd lived in Townsville for more than thirty years. We talked late into the night. He spoke passionately about his childhood on Murray Island and the court battle, which at that stage he'd been fighting for seven years. He chain-smoked throughout the entire meeting; it was a humid summer night in Townsville and the pools of smoke hung in a haze around our heads. We quickly established a liking for each other and had many a shared outlook on life. Eddie had been a staunch unionist; I had made films about the labour movement. Eddie was passionate about human rights; I was a supporter of the land rights movement. We felt comfortable with each other; I admired his intellect and his passion for social change. He was keen to make a documentary about his legal battle and we left each other that night in the knowledge that he was about to turn Australian history upside down and that I would record the process every step of the way.

With Eddie's commitment to making a film, I headed off to Britain with my business partner of the time, Sharon Connolly. We managed to get a foot in the door at Channel Four to pitch the idea of a film about the Mabo Case to their Commissioning Editor for Documentaries. We had the good fortune to meet with Peter Moore on his first day in the job. Peter, by chance, was also a lawyer. He was quickly sold on the idea and *Land Bilong Islanders* was his first commissioned documentary from Australia. With that pre-sale behind us Sharon and I knocked on the door of Jonathon Holmes, Head of Documentary at the ABC. We also found favour with Jonathon and, with these two pre-sales under our belts, we approached the Australian Film Commission and Film Victoria for production investment.

In May 1989, four months after I first met Eddie, we started filming the court proceedings on Murray Island. The Supreme Court of Queensland was visiting the island to determine the facts of the Mabo Case for the High Court of Australia. Justice Moynihan and his court toured the island and heard traditional 'oral' evidence about the Murray Island system of land tenure.

My film crew and I spent four weeks on Mer. Eddie taught us a lot about Murray Island, his people and his culture. He proudly showed us his family land, plots of earth dotted all over the island. We camped on the beach at the village of Las with his friend from childhood, Jack Wailu. They took us fishing in their stone fish traps, and sang traditional Meriam songs around the campfire. We filmed all these activities and in the process came to understand the depth and the strength of Meriam culture. The evidence was overwhelming: how could anyone deny that this was their land?

Land Bilong Islanders was a 52-minute documentary that was broadcast on ABC-TV in July1990, two years before the High Court's landmark judgement. It went to air in Britain the following year. A *Sydney Morning Herald* critic described the film as 'like watching history in the making'. It was well received by a small audience interested in Aboriginal land rights. It also toured the world's documentary film festival circuit and won an AFI Award for Best Achievement in Sound. It successfully told the story of Eddie's claims to land on Mer. But the full impact of the Mabo case was yet to come.

Land Bilong Islanders was the beginnings of an eight-year personal obsession with the Mabo case. More significantly, it was the beginning of my relationships with Eddie Mabo, his wife Bonita and their children; relationships that were to become as important to me as those of my own family. I was eventually to become known as 'Uncle Trevor' to 34 grandchildren. My partner Judy was also adopted into this huge Islander family. Every time I travelled to North Queensland to work on other films, making a stopover in the Mabo household was a prerequisite.

Tragically, Eddie Mabo didn't live to see the full impact his court case would have on the Australian nation. In late 1991 he was diagnosed with terminal cancer. Eddie was laid to rest in the Townsville cemetery, on the 1 February 1992. Five months later, the High Court delivered its historic judgement on the Mabo Case in Canberra. More than two hundred years of denial of indigenous land rights had collapsed. The land grab was over.

Over the following years my feelings for the Mabos grew stronger. More grandchildren arrived, marriages split apart, friends died, and through it all Bonita was a tower of strength and support to those involved. My relationship to her was no longer in the realm of filmmaking. We'd shared so much in our lives. However, I also maintained a professional interest in the Mabo case. I obsessively taped the evening news and clipped every newspaper article written on Mabo as the full social and political ramifications of Eddie's case unfolded.

In January 1995 I received a phone call from Bonita: they were planning Eddie's tombstone opening for 3 June, the third anniversary of the High Court judgement. Bonita's request fortunately coincided with an idea to transform *Land Bilong Islanders* into a CD-ROM, an updated version that included the High Court's judgement and the political aftermath of the case. Sharon Connolly was by now an Executive Producer at Film Australia and together we prepared a submission for their National Interest Program. A small amount of funds were made available for shooting the tombstone ceremony. The CD-ROM would contain a biography of Eddie and the tombstone opening would be an important event in the story of Eddie Koiki Mabo.

On 3 June we commenced filming at the Townsville cemetery. The next stage of this saga was about to begin. A huge crowd of family, friends, colleagues, local politicians, unionists, academics, black and white, gathered at the cemetery for the tombstone opening. The shiny black tombstone the family had erected on Koiki's grave, not only honoured Mabo's achievements; it was a symbol of hope and change. A huge feast followed the ceremony, with a celebration of traditional dancing that continued on into the night.

The following day, 4 June, another unexpected and dark chapter in the Mabo story unfolded. Morning TV and radio news bulletins across the country flashed the dramatic news that Koiki's grave had been vandalised.

It was this event more than any other that propelled me into the making of *Mabo – Life of an Island Man*. It was a critical turning point in my own life. I had never experienced first hand such virulent race hatred. I had never thought that I would see the swastika, the symbol of the holocaust and Nazi Germany, ever used so publicly and offensively in Australia. My father had fought against fascism in the Second World War and I wondered what he would have thought of this ugliness occurring in his own country. I was also shocked and dazed to see the family I'd grown to love weeping beside the desecrated grave. As a film maker, real life drama was happening right in front of me, but I was almost too ashamed to film it. I had never felt such inner conflict on a film shoot before. It raised ethical and emotional issues not only for myself, but also for my crew, John Whitteron (DoP) and Bronwyn Murphy (sound recordist). I distinctly remember John saying, 'We've got enough, I can't film any more'. But film it we did. We all knew the importance of this moment in our national life. This was the beginning of the backlash against the advances of the Mabo case and all that Koiki had stood for throughout his long career as an indigenous activist. Over the course of the next few days the Mabos, Sharon Connolly from Film Australia and I decided that we should make another film about Eddie Mabo: a film that would honour the husband and father they loved and the man who championed human rights all his short life. We stayed on a couple of extra days in Townsville ('bugger the budget'); we had more shooting to do. We filmed the tombstone being dismantled and shot several emotional interviews with Bonita and Eddie Jnr beside his father's grave.

Four months later, on 12 September, Koiki's remains were exhumed in Townsville. The family gave us permission to film the exhumation. Koiki's fragile remains were carefully lifted out of the ground and placed in a new lead-lined coffin. Again I had to face some thorny ethical issues: how far do we go with this? How much do we reveal and why? Is this simply sensationalising the story? I asked myself these questions repeatedly. But the exhumation and relocation of Eddie's remains were a consequence of racism; the same racism he'd faced throughout his life. We had to film it, if only to say, 'This is what happens when a man's grave cannot be protected'. It had consequences for our national image abroad and for ourselves as a nation. But the implications were also great for his family. It's one of the great ironies of this story that Eddie Mabo's wish to be buried on his native land was fulfilled because of the actions of his enemies.

On 18 September Mabo's coffin was flown to Mer. At last Eddie was home again. It was good to be back on Mer filming, catching up with familiar faces and welcoming people. It was an opportunity to film a further interview with his friend Jack Wailu who also appeared in *Land Bilong Islanders*. Sadly, Jack, a very frail man, died not long after.

For a generation of Australians the name 'Mabo' has become a symbol of hope. His victory in the High Court has changed the world in which we live. It has changed the legal and political landscape of Australia and set an agenda for reconciliation between black and white Australians. But in a sense his victory also reaffirmed one of the strengths of our society. After two hundred years of European occupation, our judiciary was able to correct an historical wrong by overturning *terra nullius*, 'nobody's land'. This is the legacy of Eddie Mabo, his fellow plaintiffs and a tiny island.

I don't believe that art, literature or filmmaking can actually create social change; it's people like Eddie who do that. But I like to think that *Mabo – Life Of An Island Man* has made a positive contribution towards the broad debate about indigenous rights, native title and Australian history. The film was very warmly received at festival screenings in Australia and had extended theatrical seasons in all capital cities. It won the Australian Film Institute Award for Best Documentary 1997, the NSW Premier's Literary Award for Best Screenplay and also the NSW Premier's Audio-Visual History Award. Internationally the film has been screened at major documentary festivals. I even had the pleasure of touring it throughout North American universities with Eddie Mabo Jnr at the beginning of 1998. Whilst in New York, we went to Harlem. Eddie wanted to screen the film at the Salvation Army Hall on Martin Luther King Boulevard, but unfortunately with our tight budget and schedule, we didn't have time. It would have been a great thing to do and I'm sure Eddie Snr would have smiled favourably.

The success of the film in Australia indicates that there is a willingness amongst Australians to embrace reconciliation and social justice, provided the issue can be made to touch them personally. The film has done that and I thank the Mabos for letting me into their lives.

On stage at the State Theatre for the launch of Mabo – Life of an Island Man,
Sydney Film Festival 1997.
ABOVE: Students of the National Aboriginal and Islander Skills Development
Association.
BELOW: The Mabo family, with director Trevor Graham and producer Denise
Haslem.

The launch of Mabo – Life of an Island Man, *Sydney Film Festival 1997.*
ABOVE: *The Mabo family with Margaret and Gough Whitlam and director Trevor Graham.*
BELOW: *The Mabo gals, Gail (left), Bonita, Jessie, Malita, Celuia and Bethel.*

LEFT: *Eddie Mabo Jnr speaking at the Sydney Film Festival launch of* Mabo – Life of an Island Man, *1997.*

BELOW: *Bonita Mabo and producer Denies Haslem at the Sydney Film Festival launch of* Mabo – Life of an Island Man, *1997.*

Writing the *Mabo* Script

My close involvement with the Mabo family and my familiarity with the history of the case allowed me to rapidly gather my thoughts and ideas about the structure of the film I wanted to make. But there were many aspects of Koiki's life about which I knew little or nothing. Over the years Bonita had alluded to the existence of love letters that he'd written to her while he was working in Western Queensland. But I had never seen them and indeed had been too afraid to ask. So the possibility of making a new film allowed me to delve further, to get to know Bonita's and Koiki's story, and to find out more about their lives together. I ended up staying with Bonita for a week and we'd chat late into the night about Koiki's early life and their marriage. And then one night she pulled out the love letters, which had been preciously stored away in a 1950s handbag. This is what I love about documentary: it's a socially acceptable form of sticky-beaking.

I spent a month doing further research, meeting Professors Noel Loos and Henry Reynolds, both of whom had worked with and befriended Koiki at James Cook University in Townsville. I met with his former comrades in the union movement and also members of the Communist Party who'd helped him out at various stages in his life and career as an activist.

The script for *Mabo – Life Of An Island Man* was written quite quickly over three weeks in 1996. For me, a script is a great starting point. As a documentarist, I've always-valued writing and scripting as an important part of the documentary process. With *Mabo* and the numerous other films I've made, structuring a story on paper has always helped me clarify my ideas about what it is I want to say, and how I should say it.

Some of the questions most frequently asked by my students at the Australian Film Television and Radio School, where I currently work, are 'How do you write a script for a documentary? How can you anticipate what will happen in front of camera? Doesn't it become staged if you have a script?' Whether we like it or not, scripts are increasingly becoming part of the documentary process. Broadcasters both national and international, together with film funding agencies, want certainty about the projects in which they are investing. In a highly competitive industry the reality is, if you want a documentary pre-sale, you're going to have to write a script.

Documentary is about engaging with 'the real world' of people, places, history, and ideas. It's about interpreting and documenting the 'social reality' of our lives. But a documentary film is also a narrative, another form of story telling. It's a modern answer to the ancient need to tell and hear stories. As with a dramatic feature film, or indeed a novel, a fable or a ballad, the structure of the story in a documentary is what helps hold the audience's attention. With bad structure you lose your audience. So a documentary script is a blueprint, a way of working out the essentials of the story you're telling. If you're making an historical film based on archival materials, a biography or a docudrama, then it's possible to research these stories and structure them on paper in the form of a script. If you're making a personal or essay film, then the script will be based on what it is you wish to say and the style that you'll employ. These ideas too can be scripted. But it's not as though the documentary script is used word for word during the shoot, as in a drama. It's merely a guide for the director, the crew and those who fund the film to what your intentions are as a film maker.

The well-known American documentary writer and teacher, Michael Rabiger, often refers to two different types of documentary. There are

> ... films about closed truth, whose content and form can be decided in advance of shooting. The other kind is called open truth. Here the documentary must accommodate situations that are in change and development ... [1]

Examples of what Rabiger means are easy to find in the

Australian context. The works of Bob Connolly and Robin
Anderson, such as *Rats In The Ranks* or *Black Harvest*, are made in
the *'cinema verite'* or 'observational documentary' tradition. In
these films it's not possible to predict an outcome. The story and
the characters evolve as the events unfold in front of the camera.
The storylines of their films contain Rabiger's 'open truths'. In
Rats In The Ranks, Leichhardt City Council Mayor, Larry Hand,
wishes to stand for re-election. But can he muster the crucial
votes and cause defections from the opposition ranks? It's a film
that takes 'a behind-locked-doors look at how politicians get the
numbers'[2]. People are double-crossed, arms are twisted and until
the climax of the vote at the end of the film, no one knows
whether or not Larry Hand will get the numbers. Connolly and
Anderson originally set out to make a film about the Leichhardt
City Council, but when they met their eventual lead character,
their focus changed significantly towards following his
'Machiavellian' attempts to regain the mayoral robes. The film
makers describe their own work as

> ... narrative verite. Essentially it involves unearthing a dramatic
> narrative from the long-term uncontrolled observation of unfolding
> events. We do not operate from scripts, because what we are after
> cannot be scripted. So our treatments involve no more than a set of
> applied criteria: inherent conflict, strong characters, an analytical
> framework to support the application of a wider thematic line to the
> unfolding events. As we get older our treatments or scripts have
> become more and more vague. I'm now inclined to think that if, at the
> beginning of a project, the narrative line is clear and running, then
> you're too late! When you make films the way we do, the risk of a flop
> is ever present. That's why we take so long to settle on a subject. It has
> to feel absolutely right.[3]

Mabo — Life Of An Island Man, is a film that combines both
'closed' and 'open' truths. It was possible to research Eddie
Mabo's life with his family. It was also possible to return to Mer
to conduct research interviews with Mabo's cousins and friends
he grew up with on the island. From them I discovered the
'closed' truths about Eddie as a husband, father and friend. These
research interviews gave me insights into Mabo the man —his
passions and his behaviour at different periods in his life. Given

that Koiki had passed away several years before the making of the film, it was possible to look at his childhood, his teenage years, his marriage, the final years of his life and see a progression. In charting his life in this way, I could see the development of his political outlook and his passion for indigenous rights. It was possible to understand the sense of injustice that brewed in from an early age. In linking his exile from Mer in the late 1950s to his being refused permission to return home in the 1970s, I could identify with his personal crusade for native title. And hence the first part of the film combines archival footage with family photographs, excerpts from his love letters and diaries and anecdotes about the man, most of which could be researched and scripted in advance of the shoot.

I also knew in advance that I too would be present in this film. My relationship with the Mabo family would be central to the story, and I would narrate the film. And so it was possible to write scripted sequences based on a combination of research interviews and my everyday experiences with the Mabo's at home.

It's in the second half of *Mabo* that the story contains Rabinger's 'open truths'. These are the scenes that are post High Court judgment. The story at this part of the film begins to follow the consequences of Eddie's court victory for his wife and family. The style of these scenes is more 'observational', particularly the coverage of the ceremony to unveil Mabo's tombstone and the footage of the desecrated grave the following day. The events that took place and the family's reaction to them were 'open'. We weren't able to predict, anticipate, or forecast the horror or the emotion surrounding the desecration of Eddie's tombstone. By force of circumstance and fate we happened to be there, to 'document' it. They are powerful scenes in the film where reality bites. The story further unfolds, again in an 'open' manner, with the exhumation of Mabo's remains and his re-burial on Mer. I had some idea of the depth of feeling his relocation would cause the family, and whilst filming, this emotion erupted. The last twenty minutes of the film are quite different in style to the first twenty minutes. Narration is sparse with only a few brief interviews, mostly with his family. The emotion in the latter stages of the film is heightened. I would add a third category of truth here, called 'emotional truth'. The audience engages emotionally with the story and begins to identify with the experiences of the Mabo family.

The huge advantage I had in writing this script was that two thirds of the material had already been filmed, including the drama of the desecration, before I commenced. It was simply a matter of returning to the *Land Bilong Islanders* footage from 1989 and examining the rushes for the Film Australia CD-ROM. I could then begin to piece together the puzzle – the story of Eddie's life. Further research filled in the gaps. It was then a matter of filming it. A four-week shoot took me back to Townsville and then to Murray Island.

There is a remarkable similarity between the script and the finished film – maybe not so remarkable, given the significance I attach to the scripting process. The structure of the story and the emphasis on achieving a balance between the personal and the political are the same in both script and film. Where the film deviates is in the detail. In the script I tended to over-write the anecdotes about his life. The script is also much more explanatory than the film. In editing, Denise Haslem (producer-editor) and I decided to strip the film of unnecessary information and engage our audience in a more emotional story, to move them. The material was there in our rushes and was certainly in the spirit of the written script, but it needed to be refined and Denise managed to find the right balance.

The major difference between script and film is the absence of Noel Pearson. He agreed to appear in the film, but we were shooting during negotiations between the Howard Government and the Indigenous Working Group over changes to the Native Title Act, and Noel was extremely busy. We decided in the end to restrict those in the film to Koiki's friends or family. I had also intended to use an interview with Bob Katter Jnr. from the *Land Bilong Islanders* rushes. Katter was the Queensland Government Minister for Aboriginal Affairs throughout much of the Mabo case and is now an antagonist to native title in the Federal

Parliament. But Katter's inclusion seemed to militate against the personal nature of the film I wanted to make.

The archival voice recordings of Mabo talking about his life, which are sprinkled throughout the script, turned out to be mostly unusable. These were tape recordings of Mabo in his kitchen. A brilliant activist he may have been, but as a sound recordist he failed miserably. They were largely inaudible, but were useful in giving a sense of the constant din from seven children at home. As is often the case with documentary filmmaking, when one component doesn't work something else arrives to replace it. About two weeks into the shoot, the Library at James Cook University rang to say, they had discovered some videotapes of Mabo speaking to university classes about his life and background in Townsville. These too had very dodgy sound for the most part. But we did manage to salvage enough excerpts to fulfil our intention that he should speak for himself in the film.

The other major difference between script and film, is the narration. In the script the narration is largely informational in tone, however it's essence has been translated to the screen, but far more poetically, by Jonathon Holmes, undoubtedly the best narration writer in Australia. I'm indebted to him for the emotive spirit of his fine words. His narration helps make the film story powerful.

Having bared all the secrets, it's time to read. Obviously this publication is designed to compliment, not replace, the film. But for Mabo-case enthusiasts the script does contain some additional information about the life and trials of Mabo the man.

October, 1998

1.   Michael Rabiger, 'Scripting the Documentary', a lecture at Nordisk Panorama Film Festival, 1994.
2.   Film Australia publicity flyer, *Rats In The Ranks*, 1996.
3.   Bob Connolly, letter to Trevor Graham, 1998.

MABO

LIFE OF AN ISLAND MAN

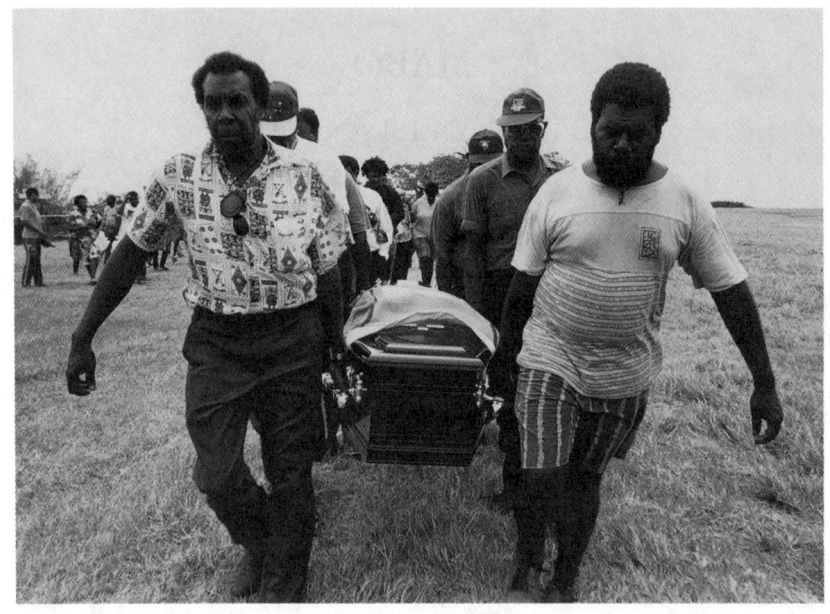

Koiki Mabo's coffin is carried across the grass airstrip at Mer. On the left Mario Mabo and right, Eddie Mabo Jnr, September, 1995.

SCENE 1 EXT. THE CORAL SEA. AFTERNOON.

Aerial views of the Islands Mer, Dauer and Waier as they rise out of the turquoise blue waters of the Coral Sea.

SCENE 2 EXT. THE AIRSTRIP – MURRAY ISLAND. AFTERNOON.

Aerial view of a small plane approaching Murray Island and landing on a tiny landing strip of grass. The plane turns at the end of the runway and taxis down the airstrip.

SCENE 3 BLACK.

Handwritten title card: 'September 1995'.

SCENE 4 EXT. THE AIRSTRIP – MURRAY ISLAND. AFTERNOON.

On the edge of the tarmac a group of islanders wait for the plane. Some of the islander men are painted up as traditional Meriam warriors. An elderly island man, Jack Wailu, waits patiently in his wheel chair. The plane taxis to a halt. From the back of the plane a shiny new coffin is unloaded and carried to the mourning party where it is handed over to the Meriam warriors.

At the centre of the mourning party is Bonita Mabo. She's wailing and sobbing loudly, comforted by her daughter Celuia and other family members. The scene is silent, solemn and emotional.

The warriors carry the coffin across the airstrip, leading a procession of grieving Murray Islanders. Fade to black.

Fade up: superimposition of a Torres Strait pigeon flying in slow motion, a swimming Torres Strait reef shark, and the figure of the turtle-shell Malo mask. Music: Murray Island sacred Malo song.

SCENE 5 BLACK.

Handwritten title card: 'MABO, Life of an Island Man'.

SCENE 6 EXT. THE SHORELINE – MURRAY ISLAND. LATE AFTERNOON.

A row of tall palm trees sway against a bright blue sky. Raging surf breaks along the home reef at Las village. Beyond the breakers the horizon line is completely empty. Koiki Mabo, wrapped in a bright red lava lava, is wandering through the shallow waters of a fish trap at low tide. He's carrying a long turtle spear and occasionally bends down to pick up shells from the water. It's late afternoon, he's lit by faint sunlight, the sky is a soft pastel blue. The sound of the breaking surf rages in the background.

KOIKI: [*voice over*] Hi, my name is 'Edward Mabo', but my island name is 'Koiki' and that's how my family and friends call me.

TREVOR: [*voice over*] I first met Eddie Mabo in 1989; we made a film together then about the struggle for land rights on Murray Island, his ancestral home. At the time few outside Australian legal circles had heard about the Mabo case, but it was soon to become the most dramatic court case in the nation's history.

KOIKI: [*voice over*] My family has occupied the land here for hundreds of years before Captain Cook was born. They are now trying to say I cannot own it. The present Queensland Government is a friendly enemy of the black people, as they like to give you the Bible and take away your land. We should stop calling them 'Boss'. We must be proud to live in our own palm-leaf houses like our fathers before us.

> *Koiki, on the reef at Las, picks up a clam shell. His bare feet wade through pools of water.*

TREVOR: [*voice over*] Koiki became a friend, and for many Australians his victory in the High Court symbolised a new spirit of reconciliation between indigenous and non-indigenous Australians. But the man who launched native title also had his bitter enemies and for a small minority of Australians his legacy is clearly reviled.

SCENE 7 INT./EXT. A HIGHWAY – TOWNSVILLE. MORNING.

Driving along a six-lane highway, past modern shopping centres, McDonald's and suburban houses. The sky is large and blue. In the background are dry mountain ranges.

SCENE 8 EXT. THE MABO RESIDENCE – TOWNSVILLE. MORNING.

My car pulls up at a simple 1940s wooden house, white with red trim and neatly manicured front lawn.

I cross the lawn. There's a couple of dogs barking. I'm holding a big bunch of flowers. Bonita Mabo greets me warmly at the door with a big hug and a 'Hello darlin'. (She will probably also greet John and Bronwyn in her usual warm manner; she's told me many times they too are part of the family. This is not meant to be indulgent; rather to suggest that familiarity, personal warmth and humour are the tone of what we film with the Mabos. It means hanging around and being part of the action.)

SCENE 9 INT. THE LOUNGE ROOM – THE MABO RESIDENCE. MORNING.

The Mabo lounge room is a treasure trove of Mabo-case artefacts. There are dozens of photographs and personal mementos. Pictures of the family, Koiki, and island craft works.

TREVOR: [*voice over*] Koiki and Bonita lived in Townsville. They made their family home here not long after he moved from Murray Island to the mainland. Their lounge room was the headquarters of the Mabo case. In this room they held meetings and plotted and planned strategies.

> *The flowers I've given her, Bonita arranges in a vase, creating an elegant display.*

BONITA: He always used to say, and clench his fist, 'I'm going to win'. He'd always say that, eh. 'When we win'; 'Whenever the case is finished, we're going to win'. It was so strong in his mind. And I used to say, 'You've got to think if you don't win, it's gonna hit you like a ton of bricks'. He had that much land, you know, handed down from generation to generation, and besides he had kids too. So he didn't want to see all that lost.

SCENE 10 EXT. THE BACKYARD – GAIL MABO'S HOUSE. DAY.

Gail Mabo is playing with her four kids outside her house; she's got her youngest in

ABOVE: *Bonita Mabo at home in Townsville, June 1996.*
BELOW: *Koiki Mabo (standing right) with his father Benny, son Eddie Jnr and Emeni Akee on Thursday Island 1962.*

her arms. Gail is cheeky and funny, a real live wire.

GAIL: I remember him saying, 'I'm going to fight these bastards. They can't take my land. I'm going to win, you watch!' So we're going, 'Yeah, dad. Yeah, sure'. Be real cynical to him, 'Yeah, sure, dad; yeah, right!' 'Dad, you're on holidays now, talk about something else!' So we'd sit down and watch football together.

SCENE 11 EXT. MELBOURNE. EARLY EVENING.

Lit offices and skyscrapers against the evening sky. Close-ups of lit office windows.

SCENE 12 INT. THE OWEN DIXON CHAMBERS. EARLY EVENING.

Bryan Keon-Cohen is leaning against his large desk. He moves around a lot as he talks. His office is crammed with law books.

BRYAN: Eddie Mabo was an independent mind and was determined to pursue a course he believed to be just in law and beneficial for the advancement of his community. Amongst all of this definitely there was an element of egotism, of conceit, of self-centred devotion to the advancement of a cause he believed in and if other people didn't believe in it, well too bad. But that's the nature of this type of agitator, revolutionary, intellectual, political leader.

SCENE 13 MONTAGE.

Grainy super-8 footage of Koiki (actually Mario Mabo in a recreation). A series of jump-cut shots: Koiki, holding a child, comes towards camera and smiles. He tries to get the child to wave at the camera. Koiki dancing in a lava lava in the Mabo backyard next to the Hills Hoist. Koiki on his boat. Koiki reading a mid '60s newspaper with a Vietnam War headline.

SCENE 14 EXT. DONALD WHALEBOAT'S HOUSE – TOWNSVILLE. DAY.

Donald Whaleboat at home in his backyard.

DONALD: Koiki, even though he might fail here and there, we all knew that he's that type of person that will eventually hit the jackpot. He often used to say, 'I can speak Meriam Mer like any Meriam', and also, 'I can speak English like any bloody white man.' He would use that word, 'I can speak English like any bloody white man'.

SCENE 15 INT. NOEL PEARSON'S LAW OFFICE – MELBOURNE. DAY.

Noel Pearson in his office.

NOEL: There are indeed figures in our Australian history about whom both black and white people can be proud. Obviously Eddie Mabo must stand in that pantheon of heroes as well.

> *Other voices overlap: sound bites from a variety of sources – research interviews, radio and TV – that build a dramatic picture of the man, the Mabo case, and native title.*

SCENE 16 INT. THE ARCHIVES – THE NATIONAL LIBRARY OF AUSTRALIA. DAY.

A set of twenty archive boxes labelled 'MABO' are laid out on a table. There are personal documents, handwritten job applications, minutes from meetings, diaries, song lyrics, newspaper clippings, and a large pencil drawing of a Torres Strait pigeon.

The camera pans across the documents and comes to rest on a newspaper headline: 'Islanders take white Australia to the High Court'. The news article has a photo of Koiki smiling and has been incorporated into a placard that includes a handwritten statement to Murray Islanders imploring them to fight the Queensland Government.

Dissolve through 'layers' of writing and text highlighting appropriate lines and words. My hand and arm are seen a couple of times turning pages of diaries and leafing through documents.

TREVOR: [*voice over*] Fortunately Koiki was an avid writer of letters and diaries and he left us his own thoughts, ideas and feelings, a record of his life and years as an indigenous community leader and human rights activist. The Mabo papers record the aspirations of the public and private man and his intense regard for his homeland, and culture.

SCENE 17 EXT. LAS VILLAGE – MURRAY ISLAND. DAY.

A time lapse of clouds billowing and disappearing across the empty Las horizon line. Dissolve to:

SCENE 18 MONTAGE.

A line of text from Koiki's handwriting: 'My mother was the second daughter of my grandfather Mabo and she married a fellow …' Dissolve to:

The tides rapidly flow in and out, filling and emptying the stone-wall fish traps. Dissolve to:

A photograph: Benny and Maiga Mabo. Dissolve to:

Tilt down through the text of Koiki's birth certificate. Dissolve to:

A photograph of Benny Mabo standing on a pearling lugger with an islander crew. Dissolve to:

A photograph of Benny's lugger anchored off Murray Island. Dissolve to:

Rippling sea water.

KOIKI: [*voice over*] My mother was the second daughter of my grandfather Mabo and she married a fellow by the name of Robert Sambo and I am the last of their five children. Our mother died giving birth and my dad then handed me over to my uncle, Benny Mabo, who was the only son of Mabo, and he and his wife Maiga reared me up. My dad worked on the pearling luggers, he was a cook for the lugger crews.

SCENE 19 KOROG VILLAGE – MURRAY ISLAND. DAY.

James and Mary Rice are sitting under a shelter at their village, Korog. James is making a weiris, a sardine fish scoop. Mary his wife sits watching him working and talking, and occasionally butts in. James talks in a forceful deliberate way: he's got many points he wants to make.

JAMES: Koiki's one of my cousin brother. My mother and his mother are cousin sisters. So we are related on that side. [*Proudly, pointing at his chest*] He's *my* cousin. His natural mother was real sister to Benny Mabo. Benny Mabo haven't got any children. So he adopt Koiki from his sister to his son and he signed his name as Mabo for all the land and seas and whatever else, the reefs and right through, all the lands, the boss one is Eddie Koiki Mabo. He's one of the traditional blood, traditional blood line of Mabo. If you're not *blood* adoption, just can't come and make yourself *boss* here, no way.

SCENE 20 EXT. MURRAY ISLAND. DAY.

A view of Murray Island from Dauer. The seas swell in the channel that separates the two islands. A travelling shot across the surface of the aqua-blue water that flows across the home reef catches the surface reflections, the spray of the water and the patterns of the waves.

Audio: the sound of wind through rigging, the flap of a sail, lapping of waves against a wooden hull and the voices of small island children.

Archival footage: The Native Problem in Queensland *(1936). Small Meriam children cling to the rigging of a double outrigger canoe. They are bare chested, wearing lava lavas. The boat speeds past at a furious pace.*

A contemporary point of view, as if from a speeding boat, of Murray island and the houses along the beach front village.

KOIKI: [*voice over*] I was like a little primitive lad growing up in a tribal situation, with very little in terms of money; the only thing we did have was the land, to support the family. And of course we had an advantage because of the fact that we owned quite a lot of land and we could grow our things that would last for months, for the whole year, and of course traditionally that was wealth.

SCENE 21 EXT. LAS VILLAGE – MURRAY ISLAND. LATE AFTERNOON.

Koiki and Jack Wailu are building a bamboo fence at Las in the late afternoon sun. Dogs are playing on the beach, Eddie Mabo Jnr and the Wailu boys are helping erect poles for the fence. Off in the distance a woman wades through the water picking up shells. Jack and Koiki confer with each other about the placement of the poles.

TREVOR: [*voice over*] When we were filming with Koiki he took us to Las, the place where he grew up with his adopted family on the eastern end of the island. He showed us his family land which had been unoccupied since his father and mother died. He and Bonita were planning to move back to the island and rebuild on land which, he said, his ancestors had occupied 'since time immemorial'. We camped with him, we helped him plant trees, he sang us songs and we talked for hours about Murray Island culture and traditions.

Koiki and Jack talk to camera as they continue to build the bamboo fence.

KOIKI: We're both Piadaram clansmen; we occupy this area of Las and they done the same things over the years to protect themselves from the Sagir wind, which is the trade wind of course, and today we're doing exactly what our ancestors did. We've also seen our fathers did that as well, our fathers have done that while we were kids living here.

More trench is dug by the sons and poles carried into position. The dogs continue to frolic on the beach, oblivious to the human activity. As he talks, the camera pans off Koiki and up the bamboo fence. The wind through the fence creates an eerie sound.

The nice thing about the noise that comes from the windbreaks is what we call Watai. And sometimes the older people used to get young pieces of bamboo and they burn a hole in them and they stand them up and turn them in certain ways where the wind could get at it and it makes that kind of continuous noise. It's supposed to be relaxing; it relaxes you as you live here.

JACK: Me and Mr Mabo are next-door neighbours; we both grow here at once ['... *together*']. This area belongs to Piadaram tribe.

Waves crash against the Las home reef.

TREVOR: [*voice over*] Seven years later I spoke to Koiki's neighbour Jack about their childhood together on Mer and growing up at Las.

SCENE 22 INT. JACK WAILU'S HOUSE – LAS. DAY.

Jack is sitting in his bamboo house. He's much older and frailer, gaunt with long dreadlocks. It's a dramatic difference.

JACK: I remember, way back when we were kids, we used to play here, me and Eddie. Even now when I go down the beach here I can see all our playing, when we used to play around when we were kids.

SCENE 23 EXT. THE LAGOON – MURRAY ISLAND. DAY.

A fisherman's point of view of the surface of the lagoon, as though quietly stalking a fish. The water sparkles. A spear is thrown into the water.

Archival footage of Murray Island men with sardine scoops diving in.

Contemporary underwater footage of a school of sardines darting away.

JACK: [*voice over*] We used to go fishing outside here on the reef. Our grandfathers and our fathers used to tell us many traditional things about our culture. They would always sing out to us to come and sit with them on the bamboo fence and they'd talk to us about our traditions and culture, me and Eddie and some of our sisters too.

   A photograph: young Koiki on the beach at Mer.

[*Voice over*] Eddie the boy would take heed of what his father taught him and he would do it.

   Jack is sitting inside his house .

So me and Eddie: we spent our time together here and like all kids we had a lot of life, a lot of energy.

SCENE 24 EXT. DAM VILLAGE – MURRAY ISLAND. DAY,

George Kudub is building something or working on his land at Dam. George's village is on the beach and is enclosed, fortress like, by a bamboo fence.

TREVOR: [*voice over*] Koiki's neighbour on the other side was his cousin, George Kudub. They lived in their own village on the beach, called Dam.

GEORGE: Every little thing we do, he loved to argue with me. Well, I remember one day we sit at the beach here and we saw big travelly along the water here.

   Archival footage: The Native Problem in Queensland. *Kids with spears wade into the water.*

   Contemporary footage: waves crashing along the beach.

[*Voice over*] So I raced down and get my father's spear, see if I can spear 'em. And Koiki said to me, 'I'm a big boy, you're a small boy. I'm going to spear 'em.' Anyway, we were arguing and Koiki said to me, 'If you don't give me this spear, I give you a fist'. I said, 'All right'. I hand over the spear to him. And when he drive the spear he missed that fish. And that fish go away. He come up and stand with me. I can see his knees shaking like he do Aboriginal dancing. Anyway we walk up to Las and Auntie Maiga asked us and he said, 'I wanted to spear that fish but I missed him'. Anyhow he got a flogging from Auntie Maiga.

George breaks into loud shrieking laughter.

Archival footage: The Islanders *(1967). Model boats are sailed along the foreshore by young boys and their fathers.*

JAMES: [*voice over*] He was grown with a sea roar, 'echoes of the sea', we call it. He listened to that. When he was a little boy he used to call us 'Big Brother'. We used to make him model canoe and then sail. He was just swimming in the beach while we were sailing about. He was a little boy. And he was a very smart, smart guy. Smart boy. Smart in brains. He got all the lessons in school very fast.

SCENE 25 EXT. LAS VILLAGE – MURRAY ISLAND. NIGHT.

A fisherman casts his net in silhouette against a dusk sky. A figure walks along the beach holding a lantern as the sky begins to darken. The water at Las is a light silver blue.

Night: time lapse of a palm tree silhouetted against moving stars and clouds.

Koiki, Bonita, Eddie Jnr and Jack and Norita Wailu are eating together. The wind chimes from the fence are distinct and a gale blows through the bamboo hut. The scene is lit by lanterns.

TREVOR: [*voice over*] One night over dinner Koiki began to talk about his schooling on the island which had been administered by the Department of Native Affairs. Murray Island children could go no further than primary school. They were taught to read and write, he said, but were considered incapable of higher learning. But Koiki had a teacher whom he liked and admired.

Archival footage: The Native Problem in Queensland. *In slow motion young children run out of the Murray Island school house.*

KOIKI: [*voice over*] I had very little in terms of clothes. You used to go to school in bare body; in just a nesur … Nesur is our term for what they call lava lava. At that time I knew only little of English language, then I started to take notice because my teacher Bob Miles was interested to learn Meriam, and we sort-of hit it off. He would teach me English and I ... and I'd teach him Meriam Mir.

SCENE 26 MONTAGE.

A photograph: Bob Miles with island pupils at Yorke Island. Dissolve to:

Archival footage: The Native Problem in Queensland. *A circle of children playing on the beach.*

A photograph: Koiki about 1951. He's approximately fifteen, bare chested, smiling. He looks bright and confident.

KOIKI: [*voice over*] It took me two years to master it. Not that I consider meself very good in English, but at that time I thought I was good at it 'cause I could get myself understood. I admired very much this guy called Bob Miles. He made me appreciate a lot of things that the white man had to offer; things like music and art.

   Archival footage: The Native Problem in Queensland. *School children lined up in rows perform regimented exercises.*

TREVOR: [*voice over*] When Koiki was growing up, the Murray Island community was completely sealed off from mainland Australia. The island was classed as an Aboriginal reserve and was administered by Queensland's Chief Protector of Aborigines. The Chief Protector produced this film, *The Native Problem in Queensland*, on Murray Island in 1936, the year that Koiki was born.

SCENE 27 INT. THE LOUNGE ROOM – THE MABO RESIDENCE. NIGHT.

Film reels spinning on a 16mm projector. The light flickers through a thick pool of cigarette smoke. Projected onto a wall are images from The Native Problem in Queensland.

Close-up of a black hand holding a burning cigarette.

Archival footage: The Native Problem in Queensland. *Islanders march in regimented lines behind the Union Jack.*

From the front door of the Mabo living room some figures are vaguely discernible in the dark: a man smoking amidst pools of blue smoke and the flicker of the projector.

Close-up of the burning tip of a cigarette as smoke is drawn back and exhaled.

TREVOR: [*voice over*] When I showed the film to Koiki he laughed and said, 'The Protector was like the uncrowned king of the Torres Strait'.

SCENE 28 INT. THE KITCHEN – FLO KENNEDY'S HOUSE. DAY.

Flo Kennedy is preparing dinner in her tiny kitchen, helped by two of her children. She's cutting the head off a fish. Plates are laid on a table, pots boiling on the stove.

FLO: Living under the Protector you didn't get the freedom other people got. They even told you when to go to bed. You had to get permission to get married. When you left the island you got permission. When you wanted to go back you have to get permission. If you did something wrong you were sent away and you might never come back. It was like a penal colony to us. Oh, the Protector. You needed somebody to protect you from the Protector.

SCENE 29 MONTAGE.

Super-8 footage: Koiki sitting at the kitchen table writing. He pauses, takes a puff on his cigarette and continues. Dissolve to:

Lines of Koiki's handwritten manuscript, ending on, '... when I was 16 years old I was exiled from Murray'.

TREVOR: [*voice over*] Affairs of the heart were also strictly regulated and supervised by the Protector through the Murray Island Council. Local By-laws forbade the mixing of the sexes, even conversations between young men and women were considered shameful.

A photograph: Koiki standing on the beach with a big cheesy grin. Dissolve to:

Text from Koiki's writing.

[*Voice over*] When Koiki was sixteen years old he was charged with

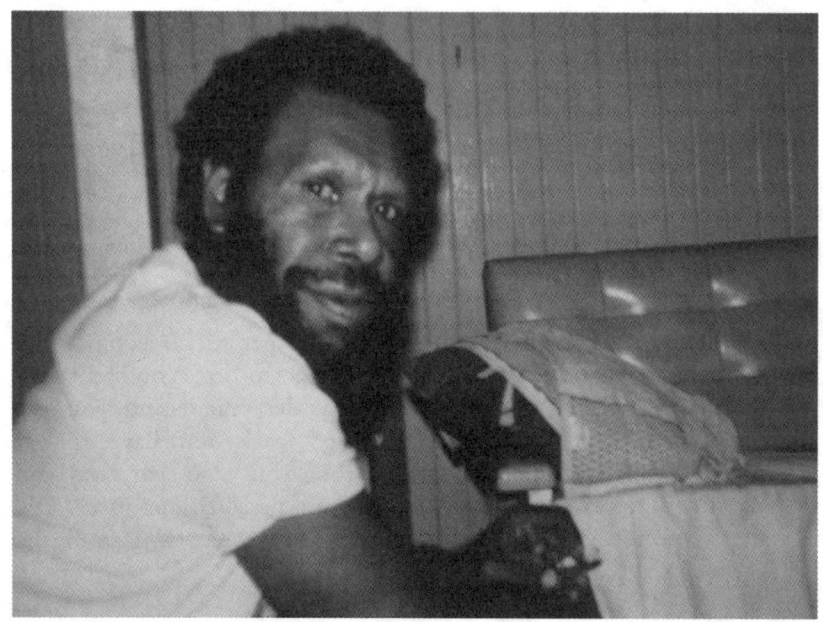

Koiki Mabo at home in Townsville, 1970.

drunken behaviour and consorting with an Island girl his own age. He was exiled from Murray for twelve months and forced to join the island pearl-shell industry as a diver.

Archival footage: pearling luggers in full sail, crewmen climbing the boat's rigging.

Contemporary footage: motion across the surface of bright blue water. In the distance is Murray Island. Underwater, looking up to the surface, the silhouette of a diver plunges into the sea and swims to the bottom in about six feet of water. The diver picks up a trochus shell and comes back to the surface.

KOIKI: [*voice over*] You'd start at six in the morning, you're wet from six until six at night, very long hours, but the life itself was good. I was a deck hand and a diver; 'swim diving' they call it, like a skin diver, but no air, just goggles. You just have to hold your breath.

Archival footage: divers breaking the surface with pearl shells.

GEORGE: [*voice over*] We went together, work in the boat. We were one crew on the dinghy and Koiki was a very frightened man for shark. He always make me to swim. I was the first one to go into the water.

Archival footage: The Native Problem in Queensland. *In the back of a pearl lugger Islander deckhands clean the shells and hold them up to the camera.* Dissolve to:

A black hand writing on lined paper with a fountain pen. Dissolve to:

Contemporary footage of a diver underwater. Dissolve to:

Handwritten words along the page. Dissolve to:

Underwater, fish, coral. Dissolve to:

Archival footage: the pearl lugger under full sail.

KOIKI: [*voice over*] I was on the Idiana for several years. It was a company boat owned by the people of Murray Island. The shell price was at its peak – it was something like a thousand pounds per tonne – but we we're being paid five hundred pounds per tonne by the Department of Native Affairs. Why should we work for half the price? I started looking at Torres Strait Islanders as a whole – as cheap labour in the pearling industry – and the other thing that worried me was the limited education that was made available to us. I wanted to get off the boat somewhere along the line and find something else.

> *Contemporary footage: the surface of the sea; the blue water and empty horizon line.*

GEORGE: [*voice over*] We were working on the boat and we were unloading shell in Cairns and he decided to run away; Koiki left me. He find a job cutting cane. We can't make money here; that's why we go mainland, for job.

SCENE 30 EXT. CANE FIELDS – NORTH QUEENSLAND. EVENING.

Dramatic cane fires in North Queensland. The fire rages, cinders spiralling into the night air.

Slow dissolve to:

Dramatic black-and-white slow-motion footage of a cane knife striking cane stems.

KOIKI: [*voice over*] Australia, the mainland, was so strange and there was unfamiliar faces and there was different language being spoken and I was a total stranger in a different environment and it was just shocking for me. I had forty pounds in my bank book and twelve pounds in my pocket. My dad had cut cane and I thought I'd give it a go. I wrote to my mum and told her I was in Innisfail.

> *Travelling shots through North Queensland cane fields.*

SCENE 31 MONTAGE.

Archival Commonwealth Film Unit footage of Cairns: the Port of Cairns, people riding bicycles down the main street, people shopping, 1950s cars. Phrases from a 1960s oral guide to Speaking Better English.

KOIKI: [*voice over*] One of the things I did when I came to the mainland, was using English, I tried to learn it as the best I could and tried to follow the Oxford system, the Oxford kind of English. And then when I came to the mainland, I discovered that the people down the streets were talking completely different type of English altogether, yeh. But I didn't lose the taste for what I call the proper

English.

Two photographs: Koiki, aged about 21, standing alone on a wharf, smiling.

SCENE 32 EXT. THE FRONT YARD – THE MABO RESIDENCE. DAY.

Celuia Mabo is watering plants on the front lawn.

SCENE 33 INT. THE KITCHEN – THE MABO RESIDENCE. DAY.

Inside, in the kitchen, Bonita Mabo is playing with her baby granddaughter. She picks her up, cuddles her, squeezes her nose, blows kisses gently on her face and rubs noses. Megan, another grandchild, is riding a toy truck around the kitchen gently crashing into walls and cupboards. Bonita's daughter Malita, is standing at the doorway having a fag. While she's playing with her granddaughter Bonita tells me how she first met Koiki. Malita occasionally butts in to rib her mum or crack a joke at her expense.

BONITA: The first time I saw Koiki was in nineteen fifty-eight. One of Koiki's relations got married to my cousin, Patsy Payne. So Koiki came for the wedding, and I could feel somebody looking at me and when I turned around it was Koiki. I looked back at him and he winked at me. And you know how girls are. And then he asked me if he can walk me home. I said no, because by that time he was drunk and so we talked for a little while and then he left.

Netta sits at her dining-room table and opens an old handbag stuffed with faded brown letters. She pulls one out and reads it to herself. Malita sits with her and reads them too. Occasionally she bursts out laughing.

And I suppose he thought he better write and apologise to me. So he wrote a letter and apologised about his being so drunk and his behaviour. I really got a surprise and we just kept writing letters.

SCENE 34 EXT. TORRENS CREEK. DAY.

West of Torrens Creek a long Queensland train slowly moves down a track. The country is parched and brown, the sky big and blue; you almost expect a tumbleweed to roll down the road.

Colour archival footage: Torres Strait Islander fettler gangs laying railway tracks between Charters Towers and Mount Isa.

Contemporary footage: shovel-loads of gravel thrown onto the tracks and a sledgehammer driving in spikes. Dissolve to:

SCENE 35 MONTAGE.

Handwritten lines from Koiki's love letters.

KOIKI: [*voice over*] 'Jardine Valley twelfth of the fifth, nineteen fifty-nine. My dear Neta, just a few lines to you and I hope that you will be glad to read it. Well I think its about time that we should call each other darling because we have known each other well enough and besides we are love for sure. Yes we are in love of course but you never tell me how you feel about me. I am asking this because I have seen a lot of girls like that'.

> *Photograph: Koiki smiling and smoking in front of a wooden church with a friend.*

'When a bloke's back is turned they start to play up, in other words muck around with some another guy and forget what they tell the joker whose back has just being turned. But "just hang on to me" please. I am running out of news so I say cherio for now and goodbye. Lots of love and kisses to you "Sugar". I remain your sincier boy friend Ed.Koiki.'

> *Photograph: a young, beautiful Bonita Nehow, aged sixteen.*

'P.S. The breaking of the waves on the shore are my love to you and the breeze on your lips are my kisses to you and give my kind regard to your mum please.'

SCENE 36 INT. THE KITCHEN – THE MABO RESIDENCE. DAY.

Bonita unfolds another faded letter from 1959. She reads to herself.

BONITA: Then he used to come nearly every fortnight to Halifax. It was a lovely feeling to be round him and Mum and Dad really took to him as well. And so that made me feel good too. I don't know whether to say love at first sight or what.

Photograph: Koiki and Bonita's studio wedding. Bonita, a white bride, stands next to handsome Koiki in a suit. They are surrounded by bridesmaids and a European best man. Photograph: Bonita in her wedding dress holding a bunch of frangipannis.

TREVOR: [*voice over*] On the tenth of October nineteen fifty-nine, Ernestine Bonita Nehow married Edward Koiki Mabo, at the Methodist Church in Halifax, North Queensland. Koiki married into a large South Sea Islander family; Bonita was one of ten children. She was sixteen and he was twenty-three.

Bonita and Malita in the Kitchen still playing with the kids. They both have a good laugh as Bonita tells this story.

BONITA: And that night he was that drunk. He was that drunk and I had to take him home to bed. I had to put him to bed and next morning I asked him about it and he said, 'Oh, how did I get home?' And he couldn't remember a thing, eh. Then we went out to Jardine Valley.

SCENE 37 EXT. JARDINE VALLEY. DAY.

Travelling shot from a train window of western Queensland bush. The landscape is stark and empty. From the front of the train the tracks disappear into the horizon line.

Music: Simple harmonica.

A long Queensland train slowly grinds its way along the tracks.

Photographs: black laborers working on the rail line. Dissolve to:

A billy boiling on a campfire in the bush. Dissolve to:

A black hand holds a Marlborough to his lips and takes a big drag. Dissolve to:

Archival footage, the rail line being built. Dissolve to:

A flock of cockatoos flying across the big blue sky.

KOIKI: [*voice over*] I learnt quite a bit about trade unions while in the railways because the fellows in Hughenden were very much in favour of trade unions and they taught me quite a few things. Although I didn't know about the art of organising a group of people together. But I started organising the gangs to come together, so we don't get shoved round the railway lines like, like they were doing to us.

SCENE 38 EXT. JACK WAILU'S HOUSE – LAS. DAY.

Jack Wailu, interviewed at Las.

JACK: If some 'big man' did something against us, Eddie the boy would stand right in front of us and say to the man, 'No, that is wrong, that's the wrong way you shouldn't do that to us'. Eddie thought he must stand up and say something about us. He used to help us when someone would growl at us.

SCENE 39 MONTAGE.

Photograph: Koiki holding Eddie Jnr. He displays his usual self confidence.

KOIKI: [*voice over*] After a while you know I kicked up a bloody hell of a stink and we went on strike. And then I found the mob rather difficult to organise because, you know, we didn't come together to start off with, as a common thing. We were all new to the area.

Music: the Mills sisters singing a traditional Murray Island Lullaby.

SCENE 40 EXT. JARDINE VALLEY. DAY.

A row of white nappies is pegged out, one by one , on a rope line by a pair of black hands. The nappies flutter against the sky and empty landscape.

SCENE 41 MONTAGE.

Photograph: a Mabo baby in nappies.

KOIKI: [*voice over*] Several times we brought our kids in to Hughenden, say Eddie and Maria for instance, when they were babies, when they were sick we'd bring them into the doctor.

Photograph: Bonita holding Eddie Jnr.

[*Voice over*] When it was too late to get back that night, we had to go to the nearest pub or whatever and ask for a room, just for the night. And we used to get knocked back; all of the pubs didn't take us.

Photograph: Bonita, the young mother, with laughing Eddie Jnr.

[*Voice over*] Probably they thought we'd leave our black skins on the sheets.

He laughs.

[*Voice over*] And even though it was winter, and you know how cold it gets out there, we would sleep at the railway station, on the platform with two kids.

Photograph: Eddie Jnr at 23 months and Maria at five months at Marathon Siding. Photograph: Malita in her frilly baby clothes.

[*Voice over*] So I looked around for another job and that's when we came back here to Townsville. Eddie was about three year old.

SCENE 42 EXT. THE STRAND – TOWNSVILLE. DAY.

Driving through Townsville along The Strand, overlooking the sea to Magnetic island; along Ross River Road; past the Townsville Harbour.

Archival footage: Four Corners *(1972). Townsville, Australian Workers' Union Hall, St James Anglican Cathedral.*

Henry Reynolds is interviewed in a park on The Strand, overlooking Magnetic Island.

HENRY: I was first aware of Eddie through his association with the trade union movement. And he had been in Townsville a few years then, and we'd been here about eighteen months. And it was then very much more typically a Queensland country town. The Aboriginal community had just, to some extent, been moving into the town, but also the first of the Islanders were coming into Townsville. And Eddie was one of the first to come here and over the next ten years I had a lot to do with him.

Archival footage: This Day Tonight *(1967). Two girls are interviewed in a cinema queue.*

FIRST GIRL: Aborigines have a separate door here and sit in a separate section, except for two of them who are better behaved than the rest.

SECOND GIRL: I think this is fair enough, because some of them are nicer than the rest.

HENRY: The white community was very much still tied to the past. People quite genuinely believed that race was an important category, that Aborigines in particular were inferior, that they had smaller brains, that you could never do anything with them. The Islanders in a way were better off because universally people thought they were 'more intelligent'. People would say, 'Oh, I can't stand the Abos, but the TIs are all right'. There was a certain amount of paternalistic affection for the TIs, as they were called.

SCENE 43 INT. THE DINING ROOM – THE MABO RESIDENCE. DAY.

Bonita, Celuia, Malita and grand daughter Megan are looking through some family photo albums laid out on the dining-room table. Other photos are in old biscuit tins and cardboard boxes. There's hundreds of them. The women are chatting about them and also having a good laugh at some of the old pictures. Bonita points out a photograph of Koiki when he worked at the Townsville Harbour Board. In the photograph Koiki has a beard and is sitting on the patio at home.

SCENE 44 EXT. THE BACKYARD – THE MABO RESIDENCE. DAY.

Super-8 footage (a Kodachrome look: intense colours): Koiki (played by Mario Mabo) is pushing young Eddie on a swing in the backyard. Super-8 footage: Koiki playing harmonica.

BONITA: [*voice over*] When we moved to Townsville he got a job down at the Harbour Board. He was working on a tugboat as a deckhand and that's when he really got involved with the unions. He used to go and listen to the Labor Party speeches and he had a few friends in the Labor Party and he became really interested in politics; you know, like party politics, and he'd go to all these meetings.

Colour archival footage, an early '60s May Day parade, placards are carried through the streets about banning the bomb.

KOIKI: [*voice over*] I mentioned earlier in one of the other tapes that we went for a walk down Flinders Street. I think it was election time, and we listened to some of the people talking, and Eddie Holbron, member of the Communist Party, got up and spoke and I sort of took interest in his speech. I really admired anyone who could speak in front of a crowd. Then the Communists would have their conferences and they'd ask me to go. It was a big step from the little island in the Straits to here.

SCENE 45 EXT. THE BACKYARD – NOEL LOOS'S RESIDENCE. DAY.

Noel Loos is standing in his backyard in Townsville. He's wearing his big broad-brimmed hat.

NOEL: One of the things about the Communist Party and the trade union movements: he used to go there just to hear good speakers. He loved oratory. And he went to one meeting because he'd heard that this senior person in the Communist Party was coming up and he went to see him speak because he'd been told he could speak for so long without using the same word twice. The importance of mastering English was important to him; that meant he could communicate across cultures, it meant that people of his generation used him as a spokesperson, because they couldn't communicate as effectively as he could.

SCENE 46 MONTAGE.

Archival footage: a union meeting where the vote is unanimous, with a show of hands. Townsville wharves, railway workers, images of working-class action and solidarity.

HENRY: [*voice over*] Townsville had been a very radical working-class town, with a powerful union movement, and some of the key unions were run by Communists, who were very influential in the town. They had been the one party in Australia – the one political group in Australia from the nineteen thirties – that had quite openly talked about racial equality, had talked about land rights, had talked about even national sovereignty for Aboriginal people. If you wanted to get something done in those days in Townsville, they were good people to know.

> *Communist Party pamphlets from the 1960s about Aboriginal rights. Photograph: wharfies carrying a banner saying 'Wharfies support equal rights for Aborigines'. Newspaper headlines from the* Tribune *proclaiming, 'Human Rights For Aborigines'.*

KOIKI: [*voice* over] I was becoming outspoken because when I used to attend the Trades and Labour Council meetings they used to say to me, 'Any issues that you think that needs to be raised, you say them and don't give it to us to say it. You've got to say it'. I was a little bit reluctant and a bit shamed to speak. They'd give me a nudge to say things and I gained more confidence as I went along. I realised they were members of the Communist Party but it didn't make any difference to me because I was treated as one of them. Actually they made me fight my own battles.

> *Photograph: Koiki sitting on his patio at home. He looks like a Torres Strait Che! Archival footage: 1967 Referendum Campaign. The campaign for the Aboriginal right to vote and for Commonwealth control of Aboriginal issues. A series of street vox pops.*

WOMAN: Some of them are too white to be classified as Aborigines, but they should have their rights.

MAN: The Aborigines behave well and they should have the right to an education and access to all facilities.

TREVOR: [*voice over*] In nineteen sixty-seven Koiki campaigned in Townsville for the Commonwealth Referendum on Aboriginal Rights. Ninety percent of Australians voted 'Yes', giving blacks in all States and Territories the right to vote for the first time. The Referendum also gave power to the Commonwealth to legislate and administer Aboriginal and Islander affairs and to include them as citizens in the National Census. The high 'Yes' vote raised expectations for some that the Commonwealth Government, with its new powers, would address the issue of Aboriginal Land Rights. Never one to rest on his laurels, Mabo wanted to push the success of the Referendum one stage further. He initiated in Townsville an interracial seminar and urged the organisers to address issues of employment, housing, education and civil rights for indigenous Australians.

SCENE 47 EXT. THE BACKYARD – NOEL LOOS'S RESIDENCE. DAY.

NOEL: They got a wide spectrum of people from the Townsville community to be involved in this inter-racial seminar. And the people they got were from churches, the trade unions, from the academic community especially and that's where I met Eddie, we were both on the organising committee.

SCENE 48 INT. THE NATIONAL LIBRARY OF AUSTRALIA. DAY.

I am sitting at a desk reading a pamphlet on the 1967 Inter-Racial Conference titled, 'We The Australians: What Is To Follow The Referendum'. On the cover are two hands, one black and one white, reaching out for each other. My hand opens the booklet and I browse through the pages. Dissolve to:

SCENE 49 MONTAGE.

Archival footage: Aboriginal and Islander dancing. Dissolve to:

Newspaper headlines on the conference: 'White Politics And An Inter-Racial Seminar'; 'Aboriginal Race Clash Ahead Seminar Told'; 'Aboriginal Laws Similar To Gaol Rules'; 'Full Rights For Aborigines'; 'Federal Attitude To Aborigines Unstable'; 'Racial Seminar Well Supported'; 'Native Speakers For Seminar'.

NOEL: [*voice over*] He suggested that we ought to have a conference to get people in Townsville to come together, to focus on problems and challenges facing Aboriginal and Islander people, and to meet together to discuss them. And this would probably be the first time this had happened in Townsville, where a large group of Aboriginal and Islander people sat down and discussed as equals with whites. He realised as a result of the conference there were two groups of people who could be useful allies: people in the trade union movement and some people in academia. So he got on very well with people like myself, Henry Reynolds and Margaret Reynolds.

SCENE 50 EXT. THE CAMPUS – JAMES COOK UNIVERSITY. DAY.

A gardener drives a lawn mower across the grounds of the university.

TREVOR: [*voice over*] Not long after the Inter-Racial Conference Koiki joined the staff of James Cook University as a gardener.

SCENE 51 EXT. THE STRAND – TOWNSVILLE. DAY.

Henry, interviewed on The Strand, Townsville.

HENRY: He spent a lot of his time in the university library and we'd spend a lot of time together over lunch talking about Murray Island and traditional societies. When you sat down and started talking about basically intellectual things, his whole face would light up. This was what really interested him. The fact he hadn't had a formal education, didn't have a degree or a PhD doesn't stop you being intellectually inclined. He was a thinker and a person who realised the importance of culture in life. So in that sense he was an intellectual.

SCENE 52 EXT. THE BACKYARD – THE MABO RESIDENCE. DAY.

In the backyard numerous grandchildren play on the swings. Inside the house Celuia and Eddie Jnr play cards at the dining-room table. Bonita plays on the couch with a grandson or daughter. The TV is on: a midday show is playing.

TREVOR: [*voice over*] Koiki and Bonita bought their house in Townsville in the early sixties. They eventually raised seven children of their own, as well as adopting three more, island style, from their extended family.

SCENE 53 MONTAGE.

Photographs: the Mabo children at successive ages, both group photos and individual.

GAIL: [*voice over*] There's Eddie Jnr, oldest boy, and then there's Maria Jessie, who is oldest girl. Bethel, she's the next one, then there's me, middle one. Then comes Mal, then Malita, then Celuia. Then there's Mario and Wannee, and they're adopted into our family through Dad, by his younger sister who passed away at childbirth. Then we adopted Ezra into our family, who was our nephew; he became like a brother, a younger brother that we didn't have. And then that's all the members of our family.

SCENE 54 MONTAGE.

Super-8 footage: Gail Mabo playing with her four kids outside her house.

GAIL: [*voice over*] Growing up in the Mabo family was … a lot of squabbles, family squabbles. Lots of bickering between sisters and bullying with brothers and older brother used to bully, and then Dad used to chastise him and then if we bullied, well Mum used to chastise us. And then if we all squabbled, well then we all got flogged. That was end of story, no one did anything wrong then. We were all good.

Super-8 footage: Koiki and young children in the backyard next to the clothes line. He's dancing and the kids are copying him.

Super-8 footage: Koiki playing island drum and singing and the kids dancing.

BONITA: [*voice over*] He was a strict father. And he really loved the kids. He would act the goat with the kids and have fun. And the kids could do the same back to him, like they do now to me. You heard them. Well, this is how they used to treat him as well. But then there was this time when he was — had his serious moments. And the kids knew not to say anything that would upset him, otherwise they would have been in strife.

> *Early to mid '70s TV archival footage: a fast montage including the election of the Whitlam Government, the coup in Chile, Nixon's impeachment, the West Indies' cricket team winning their first World Cup, the fall of Saigon, Whitlam sacked, the* Four Corners *logo.*

EDDIE JNR: [*voice over*] Every Sunday at Hibiscus Street for as long as I can remember there was always a roast dinner; everyone was home and after lunch *Four Corners* was on: all of the news-type stories, politics and everything like that would come on. So every week we started talking politics. He'd sit there and talk to the TV sometimes. And then he'd look around at us as if, 'Yes, aren't you in this conversation?'

SCENE 55 EXT. THE FRONT YARD – THE MABO RESIDENCE. NIGHT.

Night: the lights are on in the Mabo house. Through the front door you can just make out the flicker of the TV and hear a blues track.

SCENE 56 INT. THE LIVING ROOM – THE MABO RESIDENCE. NIGHT.

Inside, the living room is dark and smoky. Details are lit: wedding and family photos, island craft works. A black hand rests on the edge of the couch, holding a burning cigarette.

GAIL: [*voice over*] He loved to listen to blues … because in blues they talk about the hard life. He'd really listen to the lyrics and listen to what people were trying to get across. And I remember him sitting there and just listening.

SCENE 57 EXT. THE BACKYARD – GAIL MABO'S HOUSE. DAY.

Gail finishes the story with big gestures.

GAIL: Mum was into different things: she was into country-and-western. You'd have Dad and his old, you know, Blue Eyes singing out of this side, and Mum would have country-and-western down the other end. And then in the middle were us, with our, you know, seventies disco music.

SCENE 58 INT. THE GYMNASIUM – A TOWNSVILLE HIGH SCHOOL. DAY.

Gail Mabo is teaching her dance class. About thirty teenage Aboriginal boys and girls go through their paces in a large modern gymnasium. Halfway through their routine Gail stops them. Some of them have got their steps wrong and she runs through those bits of the routine. She is strong and assertive and in command of this large group.

GAIL: [*voice over*] Intense, passionate; if he was determined to show you something, he would. Any occasion, he'd get up and dance and sing. And that's how we grew up. If Dad had a couple of drinks he'd just get up and he'd be bending down like them island men and he'd be just dancing and singing and say, 'Come on, get up, you kids'. And we'd have to drop or stop whatever we're doing, get up and dance with Dad. Or if he'd say, 'Okay, you girls, we're going to learn how to waltz'. He'd waltz us around the lounge.

SCENE 59 EXT. THE BACKYARD – GAIL MABO'S HOUSE. DAY.

GAIL: He'd move all the furniture out of the way and he'd put an old Dean Martin record on, or you know, Bing Crosby or something, and then we'd waltz. He'd say 'I'm going to teach you girls how to waltz'. He said 'There's no good woman if they can't waltz'. And I said, 'What about the boys, Dad?' And he said, 'Oh, the boys are busy'. And I thought, well, the brothers can't waltz now, they don't know how. And the girls were taught by the best because Dad was really light on his feet.

SCENE 60 MONTAGE.

Archival footage: The Islanders. *A black band sings 'Chica Chica Chi Chi' and 'Tutti Frutti', Island style. The hall is crowded with Island couples dancing cheek to cheek.*

BONITA: [*voice over*] When we shifted here he started off with the different organisations. First the Aboriginal Advancement League. Every weekend we used to run dances for fundraising to send people down to Canberra, to go and talk with the ministers, to try and get funding. We used to get bands for dances and that.

SCENE 61 INT. THE NATIONAL LIBRARY OF AUSTRALIA. DAY.

Documents from the Yumba Meta Housing Association. My hand flicks through some of the correspondence.

TREVOR: [*voice over*] In nineteen seventy-five Koiki became the President of Yumba Meta, a housing co-operative that purchased houses in Townsville with Commonwealth funds and rented them to Aboriginal and Islander tenants.
BONITA: [*voice over*] When he got in as president, he started to look through the files and he noticed a lot of things were missing and not there.

SCENE 62 INT. THE KITCHEN – THE MABO RESIDENCE. NIGHT.

Eddie Jnr and Bonita are in the kitchen. Bonita chops up food for dinner.

BONITA: There were people that far behind in rents that they ended up going to court. Koiki took them to court and so they were evicted. But they wouldn't pay their rent or anything into the organisation; some of them were over two thousand dollars behind in rent. He ended up putting people out on the streets.

SCENE 63 MONTAGE.

Newspaper headlines and photographs from Yumba Meta file: 'Evicted Family Of 6 Stranded In Bush', 'Election Widens Housing Rift', 'Mabo: Tenants Group Illegal', 'Friction Between Aborigines, Islanders Worry', 'No Rift Between Ethnic Groups, Says Spokesman'.

BONITA: [*voice over*] And he used to get a lot of threats and had a lot of enemies because of his mouth. He wouldn't shut up to anybody, and more if he knew he was right.

> *Photograph: Eddie looking defiant.*

EDDIE JNR: [*voice over*] I remember Dad blowing out one night. Stressed to the max. Politically things … Well, this was a taxing time and he lost it. And he was just breaking things in the house; almost trashed the house. And I know now what was going on – the political climate in Townsville at the time was the big blow out – but at the time I didn't know what was going on; gone mad or something.

SCENE 64 INT. THE DINING ROOM – THE MABO RESIDENCE. NIGHT.

In the dining room Bonita, Eddie and who ever else is there, are having dinner.

BONITA: [*voice over*] We had our ups and downs like any other marriages. When Koiki saw things down the street – like if anything happened to the blackfellas, they were getting treated badly – that would make him angry. If he'd get upset at work, well, he comes home and I'm the nearest one there, so he takes it out on me. I got up and I left him but always came back again. After a while he sort of started to realise that he did have a bad temper and he got to control it.

SCENE 65 MONTAGE.

A painting: one of Koiki's self portraits.

GAIL: [*voice over*] When he was stressed he'd draw and he'd paint. I'd go and watch him when he was doing a self portrait. I said 'What are you doing, Dad? Anyone would think you loved yourself, sitting in front of the mirror.' He said, 'Well, this is the only way I'm going to do a self-portrait. How else am I going to do it?'

> *Koiki's paintings, sketches and watercolours: all of them depict scenes of Murray Island.*

[*Voice over*] He'd go out and buy all these little pieces of masonite and paint them up and sit there for hours and paint and paint and paint. And he'd paint things he remembered, like Murray Island, and the shape of Murray Island and things around, all the things he wished were there and stuff like there'd be really big palm trees leaning over the water.

> *Super-8 footage: Koiki sitting at a table on the patio writing. He looks around at camera. Dissolve to:*

> *Slow-motion images from Murray Island, past and present: the reef at Las, pearling luggers, sardines underwater, swaying palm trees, men diving in the water with sardine scoops.*

GAIL: [*voice over*] He was thinking about his family, and that he'd like to be there and stuff. I knew he was always homesick.

DONALD: [*voice over*] He would just burst out crying if he talked about Murray Island. When you talk about your island and where you come from, everything comes into it: you remember about how your father would come to you through the wind, and what your totem is. How you can be in touch with your ancestors, even though they are passed on. You can still feel their presence through some of the totems, whatever your totem might be. If the wind is blowing, everything stops because that's your totem and your family has come to visit. Your family's here. You allow the wind to rub against your face, because that's your father; the spirit of your father is rubbing his face against yours.

SCENE 66 EXT. THE BACKYARD – DONALD WHALEBOAT'S HOUSE. DAY.

Donald is standing in his backyard in suburban Townsville.

DONALD: And that's what Koiki felt even though he was in Townsville for so many years away from the island; that's what I feel, I think that's what all Murray Islanders feel, even though they are here.

SCENE 67 MONTAGE.

Archival footage: a black-and-white video from the Black Community School, Townsville. Koiki Mabo is seated amongst a group of young Islander children. He's singing and performing 'Ta Ba Na' a sit-down Island dance.

TREVOR: [*voice over*] Koiki's greatest achievement in the seventies was to establish the first independently run black community school in Australia. Based in Townsville, Mabo was the school's director. Even when pregnant and caring for five children, Bonita played a major role at the school, while Koiki sought students and funding.

   Archival footage: kids at the school engaged in craft activities.

KOIKI: [*voice over, from the video*] The children of the Black Community School are having a craft afternoon; the teachers' aid is Mrs Dolia. The rest of the kids with Mrs Mabo are also doing craft work. They seem very happy, particularly when they're doing craft work. We only have a limited number of children here, but they are a tightly knit group. And they are happy in their work and happy at the school as well.

DONALD: [*voice over*] Koiki said to me, 'We need to be able to teach our kids our culture, otherwise we will lose it because there's nothing of the Islander culture in the white school'. And he said, 'If culture is not there, the identity will be lost as well'. And he said, 'Do you think you'll be able to bring your kids over there?' So my kids went into the Black Community School. Then I was surprised to see my kids were able to do the island dance.

   Photographs from the Black Community School: kids in the classroom and playground.

HENRY: [*voice over*] They were doing what Greeks and Turks and everyone else does. That is, they set up a Sunday school, or a

ABOVE: *Children at the Black Community School, Townsville, 1973.*
BELOW: *Koiki Mabo and children at the Black Community School, 1973.*

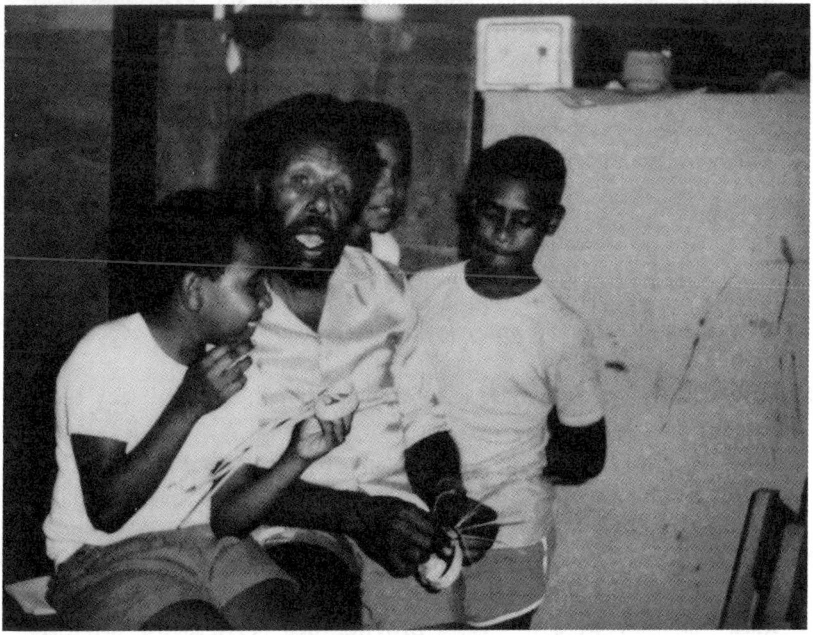

Saturday school, to give the kids the culture and the language. It's the classic problem of the immigrant. You can't bring your whole culture with you; you can only bring a certain amount.

Video images of the school. Pinned to the board is the drawing of a man with body parts written in Meriam Mir.

KOIKI: [*voice over, from the video*] Parents' participation is welcomed here at our school. The school you are watching is the only black community school run by black people themselves in Australia. There is a vast difference in attendance of the children here in comparison to the normal state schools, because they know it's their school. It's been set up by these kids' parents.

SCENE 68 EXT. INNER CITY TOWNSVILLE. DAY.

The contemporary exterior of the building at Nelson Street. Cars flash by.

Audio: a track from 1974 of the Black Community School children singing.

NOEL: [*voice over*] The community school was right in the heart of an urban area, where there were schools all around it. And therefore it was in a way an affront and a challenge to the existing school system. It was saying very clearly, 'We don't think you're doing well enough. We want our own school', and that was how it was taken: as an insult to the white education system, which of course had been failing and failing and accepting the fact that Islanders and Aborigines could only achieve a very limited degree of education.

SCENE 69 MONTAGE.

Photographs and video images of non-indigenous teachers.

Archival audio: an ABC radio interview with Koiki Mabo by Matt Peacock.

MATT PEACOCK: [*voice over*] Is it a problem that there aren't any black teachers?

KOIKI: [*voice over*] Yes, there aren't any blacks with school-teacher training. There's only one black in Australia who has graduated from university!

NOEL: [*voice over*] It wouldn't have probably started had they not run into some dedicated school teachers who were so caught up by the idea, that they were willing to provide their services for whatever was going as far as salaries were concerned. Often it was half pay.

HENRY: [*voice over*] It was strongly opposed, of course; not just by the Education Dept and the general white community, who said it's apartheid, but of course by many Aborigines and Islanders. Aborigines who said 'Look, you know, we spent all our life getting away from special blackfella schools. We want our kids to have the real thing.

> *Archival footage:* Four Corners *(1972). The Universal World Church. Islanders sing in a fundamentalist style. The Minister Dr Nielson is dressed in highly ornate robes. Members of the congregation clap hands to music. Black hands play bongo drums. Choir members sing and clap.*

DONALD: [*voice over*] At that time most Islander families here in Townsville, all the Islander families who work on the railways, joined the Universal World Church. And with the doctrine of the Church they were against people doing Island dancing. They said that is too worldly. So all the Islander families none of them were performing any Island dance or any cultural thing here in Townsville.

> *Photographs: Koiki and Black Community School kids performing Island dancing.*

Then Koiki started to perform with the Black Community School kids and when they first performed the dances everybody was shocked. Islander people in that Church were saying to me, 'Look don't hang around with Koiki'. And these are Islander people who are relations. They say, 'Don't hang around with Koiki, because he's just come up with all these big ideas. He won't get anywhere'. And I said, 'I want my kids to learn about culture'. And you used to hear, 'But culture won't save you; get your kids educated in the proper school. Pull your kids out from there; if you die, your culture won't be able to get you to heaven. Focus more on Jesus: that's where your salvation is'.

> *Archival footage: Universal World Church. Islanders 'speaking in tongues'.*

HENRY: [*voice over*] Much of the time I think he was totally isolated from the Island community, often over the question of religion; but of course most people from the Islands regarded him as a dangerous trouble maker.

ABOVE: *Maria Mabo at a May Day march, Townsville, 1977*
BELOW: *The Black Community School bus participating in the annual May Day march, Townsville 1977.*

Children from the Black Community School participating in the annual May Day march, Townsville 1977.

Photographs of the kids and the school bus participating in May Day parades. The bus is plastered with placards: 'Aboriginal and Islander Education is Queensland's Farce', 'We Demand Federal takeover of Aboriginal Reserves', 'We Want Independence For Torres Strait'.

Photograph: Koiki standing next to the school bus.

The Islanders were fairly conservative in their political attitude. And here was this person who had gone to Townsville and was associated with dubious people and had all these new ideas and in a way they probably saw him as an absolute renegade and ratbag.

Photographs: Mabo giving lectures to students at James Cook University. He's standing at a lectern, speaking into a microphone or holding a weiris *(sardine scoop). The university lecture room is full of students. In some of the photographs he's talking one-to-one with students.*

Archival audio: Mabo's voice, amplified through a PA.

KOIKI: [*voice over*] Struggle for land rights has been a major issue for Aboriginal and Islander politics for the last decade and our struggle for land rights has attracted many of our fellow white Australians to join with us ...

NOEL: [*voice over*] I used to have him out to do lectures for me. And there were other people having him out doing lectures too: schools invited him out, and he had quite an interesting talking program.

KOIKI: [*voice over*] I don't want to be a white man and I expect you don't want to be a back man either ...

NOEL: [*voice over*] If you were looking for a prominent black activist to talk to students in Townsville, Koiki was one of them, you know. He was just on any measuring stick very politically active.

KOIKI: [*voice over*] What I know about my people and our culture did not come from any books written by academics. My text books were my parents, especially my late mother and father Maiga and Benny Mabo, and so many other people who contributed to my traditional education. My family totems are the shark and Torres Strait pigeon.

Colour photographs: Koiki singing for a large group of Islander dancers.

HENRY: [*voice over*] We would constantly talk about his land and going back to his land. And among the things I started off saying was, 'You've been away a long time. Will it still be yours when you get back?' 'Yes, yes, of course it will. Everyone knows it's Mabo land. There's no problem there. People will look after it. No one's going to take it.' And I said, 'How can you be sure?' 'It was at that stage I said to him, 'Look, you do realise, do you, that you don't own that land at all, it's all Crown Land'. And he was thunderstruck, quite staggered by this information. He was incredulous. 'Don't be ridiculous. How can you say such a ridiculous thing.' He realised that I wasn't making it up, and horrified that what I was saying was probably true.

Colour photographs: Koiki, Bonita and their kids.

TREVOR: [*voice over*] In nineteen seventy-three, the year he founded the Community School, Koiki decided to return to Murray Island. It would be his first visit to his ancestral home in fifteen years. Bonita and Koiki hoped to visit his adoptive father, Benny, who was suffering from a long illness, and they wanted the children to meet their grandfather.

A series of telegrams to and from Eddie Mabo printed out on a tele printer:

> *Eddie Mabo*
> *Townsville*
> *11th April '73*
> *PERMISSION NOT GRANTED YOURSELF AND PARTY TO VISIT MURRAY ISLAND …*
> *CHAIRMAN MURRAY ISLAND COUNCIL*

> *Chairman*
> *Murray Island Council*
> *Torres Strait*
> *15th April '73*
> *REQUEST PERMISSION TO VISIT MY FATHER. HE IS ILL.*
> *EDDIE MABO*

> *Edward Mabo*
> *27th April '73*
> *PERMISSION NOT GRANTED FOR YOUR WIFE AND FAMILY TO VISIT MURRAY ISLAND. PLEASE DO NOT QUESTION FURTHER THE AUTHORITY OF MYSELF AND COUNCIL.*
> *CHAIRMAN MURRAY ISLAND*

Bonita Mabo and the Wailu children beside the grave of Koiki's father Benny,
Murray Island, 1977.

SCENE 70 EXT. THE MURRAY ISLAND ROAD – MURRAY ISLAND. DAY.

Waves break on the shore. People stroll down the village road, kids ride their bikes along the village track.

KOIKI: [*voice over, from a radio interview*] The Queensland Government tried to block my return to the island. I've got the telegrams telling me I'm not permitted back to my own island where I was born.

> *James Rice is riding his motor bike along the Murray Island road, through parts of the village. James waves to people as he passes them on the track.*

JAMES voice over] He wanted to come and see his Dad. And they stopped him. They stopped him because we got a council law here that said no people from down south. You are non-Islanders, don't come here, even though their property was here. There were other people living on the land of those people down south and the council said those owners down south can't claim the lands even though they own it. Which is stealing. See? So when Koiki come they stopped him.

> *The gravestone of Benny Mabo in the Murray Island cemetery.*

BONITA: [*voice over*] It wasn't long after that that the old man died.

SCENE 71 EXT. THE BACKYARD – THE MABO RESIDENCE. DAY.

Bonita in the backyard with her grandchildren.

BONITA: That really affected him a lot; really bad. To know that he couldn't go across to see his father and for the children to see their grandfather, it really hurt him badly. And I think all that built up inside of him, all that anger. He'd swear and carry on, 'Nothing's going to keep me away; I'm an islander and that's it'.

SCENE 72 EXT. MURRAY ISLAND. DAY.

Aerial views of the islands, Mer, Dauer and Waier. Looking down the Mer beach to Dauer and Waier. Islander women fishing.

KOIKI: [*voice over, from a radio interview*] I finally got back onto the island in nineteen seventy-seven and was welcomed with open arms. I knew the islands were mine and no one could stop me from going there. That's what led to this case *Mabo and Others against Queensland and the Commonwealth.*

SCENE 73 MONTAGE.

Archival footage: Land Bilong Islanders. *The underwater and sardine-fishing sequence from the beginning of the film. The cast net is thrown in the water and the sardines are caught. The net is brought up on the beach and emptied.*

TREVOR: [*voice over*] In nineteen eighty-two Mabo and four other plaintiffs filed a writ in the High Court of Australia. They claimed they were customary owners of land on Mer, their ancestors they said, had occupied the island since time immemorial.

   Koiki and Jack Wailu walk along the beach at Las.

Koiki knew at that stage that the court case was history in the making. He told me he saw the case as a David-and-Goliath story. Not only was he taking aim at the Commonwealth and Queensland Governments, but also the assumptions Australians have about their history; the myth, as he called it, that the land was unoccupied, a *terra nullius,* before white settlement.

SCENE 74 EXT. WILLIAM STREET – MELBOURNE. DAY.

The statue of justice – a blindfolded woman holding a set of scales – stands on top of the Victorian Supreme Court building in Melbourne. Lawyers walk past in their wigs and gowns, in Melbourne's legal district.

SCENE 75 INT. NOEL PEARSON'S LAW OFFICE – MELBOURNE. DAY.

Noel explains the pre-Mabo legal status of Murray Island. It was considered 'waste lands' of the Queensland Government. Across mainland Australia Aboriginal people, from the time of white settlement in 1788 until Mabo, were not seen to have any rights to land. The governments of other countries such as the USA, Canada and New Zealand had negotiated treaties with their indigenous peoples, but Australia was considered by its governments to be 'terra nullius', which means 'a land unoccupied', prior to white settlement.

SCENE 76 EXT. THE INNER CITY – BRISBANE. DAY.

City streets, traffic and the Queensland Parliament. Bob Katter Jnr sits in the press gallery of Parliament House.

TREVOR: [*voice over*] The Queensland Government was named as the First Defendant in the Mabo case. Bob Katter Jnr was the Minister responsible for Aboriginal and Islander affairs when proceedings commenced.

KATTER: The Mabo case questions the ownership and the title of every single person in Australia, be he white or be he black, and there's hardly anyone pure white in Australia and there's hardly anyone pure black in Australia and thank goodness for that. But every single one of those titles is thrown into question in this case and that is really what Eddie Mabo wants. He wants the white ownership of Australia knocked on the head.

> *Koiki and Bonita are in the back of a taxi. Koiki has his arm around Bonita as he looks out the window to Brisbane's tall city buildings.*
>
> *Audio: a montage of radio and TV sound bites from the early days of the Mabo case.*

RADIO ANNOUNCER: [*voice over*] A Supreme Court judge has set a time limit of three months to complete a trial establishing statements of fact in a court case over land rights in the Torres Strait ... Eddie Mabo and James Rice say they are the traditional owners ...

SCENE 77 INT. THE SUPREME COURT OF QUEENSLAND – BRISBANE. DAY.

The Mabos, other plaintiffs and barrister Bryan Keon-Cohen enter the court building.

SCENE 78 INT. THE COURT – THE SUPREME COURT OF QUEENSLAND. DAY.

Inside the court Justice Moynihan enters the room and the bailiff announces the opening of the court. 'God Save the Queen.'

TREVOR: [*voice over*] Four years after the issuing of the writs the trial commenced in the Supreme Court of Queensland. The High Court had ordered that the facts of the case be determined in Brisbane by Justice Moynihan of the Supreme Court of Queensland.

JUSTICE MOYNIHAN: [*voice over*] My task, as I think I understood it, was that I had to determine the facts in terms of the issues that were raised in the pleadings – in the claims that the plaintiffs were making, in the context of litigation.

SCENE 79 INT. JUSTICE MOYNIHAN'S OFFICE – THE SUPREME COURT OF QUEENSLAND. DAY.

JUSTICE MOYNIHAN: At the stage I dealt with it the Mabo case was pretty specific and pretty focussed. It said, here are these people, the plaintiffs; here is Murray Island; here are the blocks on Murray Island which they say are theirs. They say they are theirs because of the system that applied on Murray Island at the time of European settlement or possession, and it continues.

SCENE 80 EXT. THE LANDING STRIP – MURRAY ISLAND. DAY.

A light plane approaches the island and lands on the tiny landing strip. Justice Moynihan and the court party climb out of the plane and are transported by tractor down the track and through the main village.

TREVOR: [*voice over*] Most of the trial evidence was heard in Brisbane. But in May 1989, seven years after the writs were issued, Justice Moynihan visited Murray Island to hear further evidence.

SCENE 81 EXT. THE CENTRAL VILLAGE – MURRAY ISLAND. DAY.

The court entourage arrives and is greeted by the Murray Island Council Chairman and Koiki's lawyers. They discuss plans for the progress of the sittings on Murray Island.

SCENE 82 EXT. WEBOK – MURRAY ISLAND. DAY.

Greg McIntyre, Koiki and young Eddie Mabo are sitting at Webok, down the end of the island. In the background are the islands of Waier and Dauer.

Eddie Mabo Jnr, Koiki Mabo and solicitor Greg McIntyre on Mer, May 1989.

KOIKI: As far as the Murray Islanders are concerned it is very exciting. We feel we have made history in terms of the highest court in Queensland coming up to an Aboriginal or Islander community to sit in our public hall and listen to us. We are happy that they have come out here, to be with us, to hear all the evidence from our elderly people.

SCENE 83 INT./EXT. THE COURT – THE CENTRAL VILLAGE. DAY.

The court session on Mer is opened by the bailiff. Up to a hundred Murray Islanders, including Koiki and Bonita, crowd out the community hall.

JUSTICE MOYNIHAN: Before we proceed with today's hearings it's perhaps apposite that I remark that this is an historic occasion, since it is the first sitting of the Supreme Court of Queensland on Murray Island. The Case is an important one, involving as it does the people of Murray Island pursuing claims against the state of Queensland and the Commonwealth of Australia. Sitting here helps me to understand the evidence concerning Murray Island, it's people and its culture, and perhaps most importantly it enables the people of Murray Island to participate in the process of justice that's being worked out in these proceedings.

Eddie and Bonita sit in court at the start of the day's proceedings.

BRYAN: Eddie was, in my experience, genuinely concerned to advance the interests of his people in regard to cultural rights and land rights. He struck me as very intelligent. He had an extremely good working knowledge of the way lawyers work, how to bridge that gap between the workings of the Australian legal system and its legal concepts and the workings of the Murray Island traditional system of land tenure and the customs of that community. That was a formidable task: explaining Murray Island to the lawyers so that the lawyers could explain it to the court.

SCENE 84 EXT. THE CENTRAL VILLAGE – MURRAY ISLAND. DAY.

Koiki stands in the village square talking to Murray Island witnesses. He explains details of the court case to them in Meriam Mir.

KOIKI: You'll be first in court. Somebody will cross examine you. They will ask you what old Marou told you and your wife. Don't speak in English, you can speak in Meriam, someone will translate what you say. Just wait outside, someone will call you in.

> *The bailiff comes to the door of the court and calls witness Sam Passi. Sam, a bit shaky on his legs, walks slowly to the court door.*

BRYAN: [*voice over*] And similarly, he could explain to the witnesses our needs and why we were asking these silly impertinent questions about things which they had known from their fathers and grandfathers from babes in arms. It must have been very confusing for them, for a bunch of white lawyers to come along and ask questions about things which were manifestly obvious to them.

> *Bryan Keon-Cohen and Greg Mc Intyre walk down the central track of the village. They are wearing their black lawyer's gowns.*

Now, that facility of Eddie Mabo to put the two cultures together was absolutely crucial. And I think I can confidently say that without him the case would never have happened, in a variety of ways.

SCENE 85 EXT. WEBOK – MURRAY ISLAND. DAY.

Greg McIntyre, Koiki and young Eddie Mabo sit at Webok, the western end of the island. Koiki and Greg hold maps of Koiki's plots of land.

GREG: We'll be attempting to prove to the court that Islanders own particular tracts of land as family groups with the individuals' heads having control of them, and so we've produced a series of maps on the basis of what Koiki and others have told us about where their particular lands are, and they're very clearly defined. One of the interesting aspects about this case is that Islander tradition has very clearly defined boundaries.

> *The court entourage prepares to travel to the various sites of inspection and are then driven to inspect plots of land.*

SCENE 86 EXT. SAUREM – MURRAY ISLAND. DAY.

The court has gathered to inspect a plot of land Koiki is claiming.

KOIKI: We're at a place called Saurem. This land came to me through my grandmother and her father. My grandmother was Akasi and her father Gasu, who owned this land initially, and this is the boundary line here. Other families have constructed these things, not just lately but over many years, to mark off their boundaries from another family; and its just small rocks that they've gotten and they picked them, piled them in heaps on the boundary lines. And this can be seen all over Murray Island.

SCENE 87 EXT. THE SEA NEAR DAUER ISLAND. DAY.

Dave Passi drives his dingy away from Murray Island, along the beachfront towards Dauer Island.

DAVE: Koiki was fighting for his pride – who he really was – and at the same time the feeling of oppression was very strong, which made him and myself really aggressive. I became aggressive; even if I was a priest, I became so aggressive.

SCENE 88 EXT. GIAR PIT – DAUER ISLAND. LATE AFTERNOON.

Dave Passi stands on the beach at Giar Pit, the sand spit on Dauer, in late afternoon sun. Behind him is Murray Island.

DAVE: We were concerned about our culture and our culture meant so much to us. It was built in us. We were threatened by the idea of crown land and so we decided to fight because I felt that we were going to lose our land if we were not careful, if we didn't fight for our land, and that's why I became a plaintiff. But I saw Koiki as the one who was leading it.

> *Koiki leads the court to another site. He charges off into the bush to inspect an ancient well site. He explains it's been there a long, long time.*

JAMES: [*voice over*] Koiki talked very hard about his traditional lands. I can see him in his role. He was good enough to speak the things he learned, not about white people's ways, but our ways, and we helped him on that side, so everything clear.

SCENE 89 EXT. JAMES' BANANA GARDEN – MURRAY ISLAND. DAY.

James sits in his banana garden making a traditional island pan flute.

JAMES: I know my boundaries I know my land. I can name them where my ancestors been name all the land. I can say this is 'Deimi', that's 'Deimi' here. If I take you to another I say 'Douri'. This is not white peoples name. This is my ancestors' name, native name and this land belongs to my ancestor and I'm the heir and that land I want to own by right I want to get rights. I'm speaking on behalf of all Murray Islanders: we want our rights.

SCENE 90 EXT. LONG GRASS – MURRAY ISLAND. DAY.

James Rice walks through long grass up to his waist, playing island pipes.

SCENE 91 EXT. LAS VILLAGE – MURRAY ISLAND. DAY.

Koiki Mabo leads the entourage down to Las and along the beach.

GREG: [*voice over*] We are essentially wanting to prove to the court that since time immemorial Islanders have owned their land in accordance with their traditions …

SCENE 92 EXT. MURRAY ISLAND. DAY.

Greg McIntyre and Bryan Keon-Cohen sit under a lean-to shelter, sorting documents.

GREG: … That there was a traditional system of rules governing the use of land, and we say that tradition carries on and contained within it are rules of inheritance.

SCENE 93 EXT. LAS VILLAGE – MURRAY ISLAND. DAY.

Koiki talks to the entourage.

KOIKI: The land usually gets passed on from father to son by word of mouth. That is our only way of passing land from one generation to the next. Before the father dies he takes his children through and teaches them where the exact boundary lines are, he would make sure that his family and friends knew his wish as to which one of his sons would be the heir to his land.

Justice Moynihan stands on the beach at Las, contemplating a fish trap and looking out to sea.

JUSTICE MOYNIHAN: [*voice over*] One of the difficulties with the Mabo case was how you perceive one culture from the point of view of another. I'm not sure that what the Murray Island culture means by land ownership, whatever that means, is what I mean or what the common law means by land ownership. The law tends to involve categorising and analysing and you've got to start wondering how much you're torturing other concepts to come within your own. For instance what would happen if it had all been reversed? What would happen if I was a Murray Island judge who was endeavouring to make findings about the freehold land system that the common law brought to Australia? You produce a bit of paper that says you're entitled to this land and I say, 'Well, our system doesn't recognise bits of paper entitling you to land'.

SCENE 94 EXT. THE SEA NEAR MURRAY ISLAND. DAY.

A dingy is travelling away from the island to one of the off-shore reefs. In the background is Murray Island. A diver plunges into the water. Underwater there are brightly coloured corals and tropical fish. The diver picks up a crayfish from the sea bottom and returns to the water surface.

TREVOR: [*voice over*] Koiki and the plaintiffs claimed that before the arrival of Europeans, Islanders had complex rules of ownership applying to both land and sea. Murray Island families and clans could own seabeds and reefs, even stars, wind and water.

Aerial views of Murray Island showing the stone fish traps that encircle the island.

They argued in court that their traditions entitled them to ownership in Australian law of seabeds and reefs which encircle the island and include their hunting grounds on the Great Barrier Reef. The Commonwealth Government, responsible for administration of the high seas and for international fishing treaties, opposed the claim to Australia's territorial waters and was the second defendant in the Mabo case.

ABOVE: *Witness Jack Wailu with his grandson on Mer, January 1989.*
BELOW: *The 'shark dance' was performed for Supreme Court of Queensland judge Justice Martin Moynihan, May 1989.*

SCENE 95 EXT. LAS VILLAGE – MURRAY ISLAND. DAY.

Koiki Mabo and Jack Wailu wade through the shallows of the reef at Las. In the background is Dauer.

KOIKI: [*voice over*] There are areas of reef in front of the area we call Las – there is a stone fish trap I'm claiming – and then there's a stretch of reef that goes out to the Great Barrier Reef. I claim that because it has special significance as far as our cultural myths and legends go. And the other thing is, while it's in my backyard, Commonwealth has no rights to send people here to harvest my sea and sell it for their benefit: that's not right. According to my tradition, those fish, the prawn, whatever is in that sea, belongs to me and my people.

> *Jack Wailu sits on the edge of the fish trap at Las at low tide. In the background Koiki wades through the shallow waters, just a tiny speck in the distance.*

JACK: [*voice over*] At night when the king tide goes out, there is no way for the fish to get out. So they end up inside the fish trap and we come along at night and spear them, They always go to the middle of the lagoon; all the fish always go there. Sometimes you can just go there and pick them up.

SCENE 96 EXT. THE CENTRAL VILLAGE – MURRAY ISLAND. DAY.

Behind the central village square a group of islanders prepare for a traditional dance. Some of them carry shark masks; others are having paint applied to their faces. Wilfred Tapau is at the centre of the group, helping them get ready.

WILFRED: We're going to perform one of our main dances. It's a shark dance; it's about our former God Malo-Bomai: he came to Murray Island shores three hundred years ago and they thought it was just an ordinary octopus, but it was Malo. He settled down here and made eight tribes on Murray Island, and this dance is one of the shark clan; so we still keep our tradition of Malo-Bomai and we're going to perform it for the judges and lawyers today.

> *The dancers perform the shark dance in the village square for the judge,*

barristers and other assembled Murray Islanders. Dissolve to:

SCENE 97 MONTAGE.

Close-up of the nib of a fountain pen writing on lined paper.

KOIKI: [*voice over*] Malo was our supreme being, our 'Augud' as we call him, before the arrival of the missionaries, and he gave us a set of rules that we have to abide by. Just like you have Christian ten commandments, about stealing, we have our traditional laws and ceremonies that we did practice.

> *Archival footage: the Malo ceremonial dance, 1898. Dissolve to:*

> *Archival footage:* The Islanders *(1967). The Malo dance. Dissolve to:*

> *The Malo dance 1995 and Jack Wailu singing.*

The missionaries did wipe out our sacred cult when they came to Murray, but Malo's Laws remain strongly in our memories; that is where we come from. I wonder how long before we can free ourselves from the Christian mentality and fear of Christ, and be our whole selves again.

SCENE 98 EXT. THE BEACH – MURRAY ISLAND. DAY.

Kaba Noah sits by the beach holding Wasikor, the sacred drum of Malo.

KABA: *Tag mauki mauki*; '*tag*' means 'hand'. '*Teter*' means 'leg' … *Teter mauki mauki*: you can't just wander across the village. This is our traditional culture. The law of Malo. You must get permission from the owner before you go catch a fish in a fish trap. It means this: *tag mauki mauki, teter mauki mauki*. It means you can't wander in the village. This is the law of Malo.

SCENE 99 INT./EXT. A HUT – LAS VILLAGE. DAY.

Koiki sits in a hut at Las with Jack Wailu. They both glow in the late afternoon Murray sun.

KOIKI: During my time of growing up I was quite young when my grandfather taught me not to walk on anybody else's properties. The same thing was reinforced by my dad who would say that you must withhold your feet from entering somebody else's property: it's against Malo's law. For instance, I recall an incident that we went to a place called Beir up on the right side of Las.

SCENE 100 MONTAGE.

Photograph: young Koiki at Las.

KOIKI: [*voice over*] Our visit there was specifically to collect coconuts, but instead of collecting coconuts I went next door and collected some fruit, *sorbi*, and of course on my return he wanted to know where that fruit came from. And when I told him I was punished for that. Sometimes they were pretty harsh, where you'd do something and get punished, get thrashed; the old man would thrash me for doing it.

SCENE 101 EXT. MURRAY ISLAND. DAY.

Greg McIntyre and Bryan Keon-Cohen sit under their lean-to shelter, still sorting documents.

BRYAN: I'm just reading a document and it says, 'The law one: *Malo tag mauki, teter mauki*'. As I understand it, that means under Malo's Law a man doesn't walk into another man's property and a man doesn't place his hands on another man's property, and this document which we got from a witness yesterday goes on to speak of twelve such short propositions. [*Voice over*] It was an item of evidence that I thought was a very important notion in their system of land law and ours. That is the notion of trespass. Here is a notion which touches upon the crucial element of native title: the right to exclude others. Malo's laws were presented to the court by our twenty-four or twenty-five witnesses to show how there was a system of rules that governed their lives, and we said this continued.

SCENE 102 EXT. THE INNER CITY – BRISBANE. DAY.

Koiki, Bonita and young Eddie walk through the streets of central Brisbane.

TREVOR: [*voice over*] Throughout the ten-year court battle Koiki spent much of his time travelling between the island, his home in Townsville, and Brisbane where all of his personal evidence was heard. Throughout much of this period he was unemployed.

BONITA: [*voice over*] At first it was hard. Mainly because he was going away so much and I was stuck with all the kids on my own. And we was paying off the house at that time and had our mouths to feed. And every cent we had, well we put it together for Koiki's fare to go from A to B, even if he had to go to Cairns to see Greg McIntyre, well he'd jump on the bus and go up.

A bus passes through frame on the Story Bridge, Brisbane.

When he had to go to Brisbane he'd jump on a bus. But because he was away so much, he couldn't hold down a job.

Bryan Keon-Cohen, Koiki, Netta, James Rice, Dave Passi and Henry Kabere are photographed by a photojournalist in front of the statue of justice outside the Supreme Court of Queensland. Intercut the action with the journalist's black-and-white photos.

BRYAN: [*voice over*] This whole litigation had been in train for four years before anyone climbed in the witness box. So Eddie Mabo's evidence had been anticipated by Queensland. They'd done an enormous amount of research. They, for example, had researched, all the social security cards of his parents to try and work out whether or not he had been named as an adopted child or just a child for whom his adopted parents assumed some sort of foster responsibly for. And they were able to put some very penetrating propositions to him in cross examination. Like, 'Wasn't it the case that your adopted mother only had you in the house so that she could apply for and receive added social security benefits from the Commonwealth? And it had nothing to do with you assuming any traditional rights or interest in land by reason that you were island adopted?' Now these are well researched, penetrating questions. They were proper questions. They were tough questions. And they had an impact.

SCENE 103 MONTAGE.

Photographs: Koiki and Bonita at the time of the Brisbane hearings. They are sitting in the foyer of the court.

BRYAN: [*voice over*] One item I very clearly recall in the trial concerned his inability to return to the island to be with his dying father: he was banned. As it occurred we obtained a tape of his dying father speaking on the island and we tendered the tape in evidence and it was played with Eddie Mabo in the court. And he wept hearing these words because it was obviously a very emotional moment. Because his father was talking about various matters relevant to tradition and customs in the case.

BONITA: [*voice over*] He'd come home and he'd talk, and like he could see a funny side to things, especially with the judges and the oppositions. Come home, and we'd talk and laugh about it. But he really took it as fun. He didn't get uptight about the judges or the opposition. I think he took it really well. And even when some of his own countrymen went on the other side.

SCENE 104 EXT. THE COURT – THE CENTRAL VILLAGE. DAY.

Islanders file out of court at lunchtime. An ABC journalist taps out a news report on a portable typewriter.

ISLANDER: [*voice over, from the radio*] Eddie Mabo claims … his claim is disputed by some one of whom gave evidence at this week's hearing … Mabo has no right to take it away from him … Land disputes have a long history on the island, which date back to the start of this century …

TREVOR: [*voice over*] Not all Murray Islanders supported Mabo's actions. His diaries reveal that he was constantly in dispute with other land owners about their adjoining boundaries and inheritance to certain blocks of land. The Queensland barristers used this traditional rivalry to bolster their case. Of the nine Islander witnesses called by Queensland, five were called specifically to dispute Mabo's claims.

SCENE 105 EXT. SEBEG VILLAGE – MURRAY ISLAND. DAY.

Marwer Depoma walks slowly across the beach at Sebeg village.

MR DEPOMA: Koiki has big ideas. He thinks he owns the beach and the reef and the village here; he's claiming the land here. No, everybody's upset. Lot of trouble now.

ABOVE: *Solicitor Greg McIntyre, witness for the plaintiffs Meb Salee Snr and barrister Bryan Keon-Cohen on Mer, during both Supreme Court hearings and filming, May 1989.*
BELOW: *The Queensland defence lawyers on Mer for the hearings of the Supreme Court of Queensland, May 1989.*

SCENE 106 EXT. LAS VILLAGE – MURRAY ISLAND. DAY.

Victor Saggigi walks through his area at Las village.

VICTOR: If Eddie Mabo wins there's going to be a war here; disputes everywhere if Eddie Mabo wins this court case. Like today we have the Queensland government here. They are like our protectors and providers. Queensland are helping us build our houses. So we worry about traditional ownership, if that ownership comes in. The Queensland Government might just let us go. If that traditional ownership come in we might lose everything.

> *In the village square preparations are made for a feast for the Supreme Court. A turtle is cut up, women peel sweet potatoes, coconuts are gathered from trees, palm leaves are laid out on tables.*

SCENE 107 INT./EXT. THE COURT – THE CENTRAL VILLAGE. DAY.

Inside the court Justice Moynihan is making a closing address to the assembled Murray Islanders.

JUSTICE MOYNIHAN: I would not wish to leave Murray Island without concluding as I began, and that is by thanking the people of Murray Island and their council for making available to us the facilities of the island to us, in order that we may sit here. Will you adjourn the court Mr Bailiff?

> *The bailiff adjourns the court and islanders file out. Outside in the square the lawyers are presented with palm frond hats. Greg McInytre and Bryan Keon-Cohen are wearing theirs and look silly. Koiki is standing with them drinking from a fresh coconut.*

TREVOR: [*voice over*] After four days on Murray Island the court moved back to Brisbane for the hearing of further evidence. Anthropologists, writers, historians and former directors of Native Affairs gave their evidence for and against Mabo and the plaintiffs.

> *The Queensland barristers are also presented with palm hats.*

Three months later Justice Moynihan finally adjourned the court to consider and write his findings. In the meantime Koiki decided to work on his boat.

SCENE 108 EXT. THE MABO RESIDENCE – TOWNSVILLE. DAY.

Koiki's boat is parked in the drive way.

SCENE 109 MONTAGE.

Photograph: Koiki in his blue work overalls, smiling, looking older and greyer.

TREVOR: [*voice over*] He'd ring me every so often with news from Murray Island, but mostly to say he'd pulled the engine out of his boat, or he was putting in a new deck. I'd ask him about news of the court case. 'Still nothing', he'd say, 'but I'm in no hurry, Moynihan's got plenty to think about'.

SCENE 110 INT. THE KITCHEN – THE MABO RESIDENCE. DAY.

Malita and her daughter Crystal, about seven years old, are in the kitchen.

TREVOR: [*voice over*] Koiki also found he had more time for his family.
MALITA: He wasn't around when I was pregnant or when Crystal was born; he was up on the island then. And then, by the time he got back here, she was six months old. Yeah, so it was a big tear session for him: once he walked in the room and seen Crystal he just bawled. I've never seen a man bawl like that, eh. We started getting really close. I wasn't allowed to stay away for the day otherwise he'd crack a spaz.

SCENE 111 EXT. THE FRONT YARD – GAIL'S HOUSE. DAY.

Gail is in her front yard playing with her three children. The fourth is in a stroller. She becomes very emotional as she speaks.

GAIL: I remember when I had Caleb, my first son, Dad came with us; it was the first birth he'd ever been to. And I remember being in labour. I was in pain, he was holding my hand, squeezing my hand and I was squeezing his hand and he was crying. He realised how much pain Mum was in having to go through child birth seven times with us and he was never there to hold her and support her and he realised how much he'd missed by coming in with me.

SCENE 112 BLACK.

A handwritten title card: 'November 1990'.

SCENE 113 EXT. THE HIGH COURT OF AUSTRALIA – CANBERRA. DAY.

The High Court building on the banks of Lake Burley Griffin.

SCENE 114 INT. THE FOYER – THE HIGH COURT OF AUSTRALIA. DAY.

Inside the foyer of the High Court the modern architecture is severe, cold and angular. Portraits of former High Court Judges hang on the walls.

TREVOR: [*voice over*] After a year of considering the facts of the case, Justice Moynihan delivered his findings to the High Court of Australia. The judge's findings presented Koiki and his lawyers with a bombshell.

SCENE 115 EXT. THE HIGH COURT OF AUSTRALIA – CANBERRA. DAY.

Bryan Keon-Cohen stands outside.

BRYAN: The judge made a finding that Eddie Mabo was not adopted to the family of Mabos, to the branch of the Mabo family to whom Eddie had claimed. That was devastating because these claims to many of the areas of land were claims by inheritance through his adopted father. Therefore he lost all those lands. So where Eddie started off with maybe twenty-five or thirty blocks of land and seas, he ended up with none. And to that extent Queensland succeeded in their attempts to diminish Eddie Mabo's credibility in the eyes of the trial judge.

SCENE 116 INT. JUSTICE MOYNIHAN'S OFFICE – THE SUPREME COURT OF QUEENSLAND. DAY.

Justice Moynihan in his office.

JUSTICE MOYNIHAN: The only Eddie Mabo that I knew or saw was the Eddie Mabo who gave evidence in the litigation, and the only things I knew about him – and I still know, for that matter – is what emerged in the course of the evidence. Now, I didn't take a very high view of his credibility. I think I said something like I wouldn't be inclined to accept his evidence unless it was corroborated by other reliable evidence. And I declined to find that he was adopted as a Mabo so as to found a right of succession. So the short answer to your question is, on the narrow one-dimensional picture of Eddie Mabo, his credibility didn't find great favour.

SCENE 117 MONTAGE.

Jack Wailu in his yam garden. Mrs Wailu and her young daughter dig up a yam. James Rice walks along a bush track. Islanders fishing on the beach. Islanders dance for Justice Moynihan. The judge and entourage walk down a track. The sequence could be compiled with dissolving text from Justice Moynihan's findings.

JUSTICE MOYNIHAN: [*voice over*] But there was a ton of evidence other than from Eddie Mabo to found conclusions about Murray Island. What I found was that collectively, and individuals among the collectivity, had a sufficiently discernible and precise relationship with land in the context of their own social structure to provide a basis for saying that their society had a system which ours should recognise. It's almost axiomatic isn't it? If you've got a small group of people stuck on an island with limited land resource, one of whose major modes of social expression is gardening, apart from that being their means of subsistence, then it would be surprising if they didn't have some sort of system which regulated the society in relation to the land. I mean, it's almost a laboratory for the exercise.

SCENE 118 INT. COURT ROOM NUMBER ONE – THE HIGH COURT OF AUSTRALIA. DAY.

The full bench of the court files into Court Room Number One. The court is opened for proceedings.

TREVOR: [*voice over*] The Mabo case was now back in the High Court of Australia. Seven judges of the court would study the evidence, hear more legal argument and determine whether Justice Moynihan's findings meant that Murray Islanders have rights which Australian law should recognise.

SCENE 119 EXT. THE HIGH COURT OF AUSTRALIA – CANBERRA. DAY.

Bryan Keon-Cohen, outside the High Court.

BRYAN: The great irony of this case is that in the end Eddie Mabo had nothing to do with it in terms of argument put before the full High Court at the ultimate hearing. He took it on the chin, accepted advice not to appeal and proceeded into the full court with a case which was fought over areas of land found on behalf of the other plaintiffs, not him.

> *Barristers make legal representations to the full bench. Paintings of former judges on the walls of the court, from the point of view of someone sitting in the gallery.*

TREVOR: [*voice over*] Koiki maintained his determination. He travelled to Canberra for the final days of legal argument, thirty-six hours by bus.

SCENE 120 MONTAGE.

Photographs: Koiki at the High Court with his barristers.

HENRY: [*voice over*] The last time I saw him – I just happened to be in Canberra and realised that it was the last day of the sitting, the last presentations, whatever they call it – and turned up and there he was. So it was most fortuitous. But, yeah, that was a very nice and emotional meeting. So we sat together while the last business went through.

SCENE 121 EXT. THE STRAND – TOWNSVILLE. DAY.

Henry Reynolds, interviewed in a park on The Strand, overlooking Magnetic Island.

Solicitor Greg McIntyre, barrister Ron Castan, Koiki Mabo and barrister Bryan Keon-Cohen at the final hearings of the High Court, May 1991

HENRY: He had that glow that he often did when he was involved in politics and ideas and being treated seriously and as a man of consequence. He glowed in those circumstances, yeah. He shone.

SCENE 122 BLACK.

Handwritten title card: 'Four months passed ...'

SCENE 123 EXT. TOWNSVILLE GENERAL HOSPITAL. DUSK.

The hospital wards glow against a deep blue sky. The hospital wing is old fashioned: a forties building with concrete balconies. From outside you can see some people standing in the windows.

GAIL: [*voice over*] I was well and truly pregnant. I was due any time. And I remember Mum ringing up and telling me, you know, 'Your Dad's got cancer.' And I said 'What?' And she said 'Yeah, he's got cancer' and I said 'Cancer of what?'

SCENE 124 INT./EXT. THE KITCHEN – THE MABO RESIDENCE. DAY.

Malita is smoking at the kitchen doorway. Bonita holds her grand daughter in her arms.

BONITA: He'd always complain about his hip and pains in the chest. But with Eddie, he didn't want to know about it. That just went on and on. Every time he went down the doctor's, they said it was arthritis. He just wouldn't go to the doctor's. And then it'd get the best of him and he'd go to the doctor's again.

SCENE 125 INT. AN EXAMINATION ROOM – TOWNSVILLE HOSPITAL. DAY.

X-rays of a man's spine and throat are placed side by side for viewing on a light box.

SCENE 126 INT. A CORRIDOR – TOWNSVILLE HOSPITAL. DAY.

The corridors of Townsville Hospital are shiny and clean. A trolley is pushed past and along the corridor. *Footsteps on lino echo through the ward. Nurses are seen at the end of the corridor.*

BONITA: [*voice over*] Finally they did X-rays and blood tests and the next day they put him in hospital.

SCENE 127 EXT. GAIL MABO'S HOUSE – TOWNSVILLE. DAY.

Gail is out the front of her house.

GAIL: [*sobbing*] And Dad was talking like this. He had cancer of the throat. And I said, [*in a soft, croaky voice*] 'Dad how you doing?' I was mocking him. Because I didn't know how far it was gone and so I was just mocking him and making him laugh so I could hear him laugh. He said 'Gail, stop mocking me'. And I'm going, 'But Dad, this is how you're talking to me. I'm talking to you back like this'. They found out properly that he had cancer of the throat and the cancer in his hips.

SCENE 128 INT. A HOSPITAL WARD – TOWNSVILLE GENERAL HOSPITAL. NIGHT.

From the point of view of a bed. A curtain is pulled anonymously around. The scene is shot at three frames per second and step printed to produce a blur and staccato movement.

SCENE 129 EXT. TOWNSVILLE GENERAL HOSPITAL. NIGHT.

The ward lights are on. Cars flash past the hospital intersection. The scene shot at three frames a second, step printed.

KOIKI: [*voice over*] Tuesday the thirty-first of November. Netta, Selena, Maria came to see me at Ward 4HB Townsville General Hospital. They stayed until ten p.m. After they left, the rest of the night was not so bad. Back was aching.

SCENE 130 MONTAGE.

Close-up, a morphine drip.

The wave patterns of a heart monitor. Dissolve to:

Koiki's shaky writing in his diary: the date and key words.

KOIKI: [*voice* over] I layed in bed thinking about future and how I
    would like it to be, even if I am not there.

> *Dreamlike images of Murray Island. In slow motion a net is thrown into
> the water. Underwater images of fish and sardines.*

I thought about the struggles I've been through over the past years,
since nineteen sixty-three to nineteen ninety-one or to the beginning
of nineteen ninety-two, while the rest of black Australia awaits with
me for the High Court decision to be brought down at any time.
Will it be in time for me to receive it?

> *Slow motion images of Bonita and the kids, intercut with family
> photographs and super-8 footage.*

I also thought about how my wife, the most important person in
my life, has stuck to me over many hardships and hurdles in life, but
somehow we made it, perhaps better than others. To me my wife
has been the most adorable person, a friend also, a most wonderful
lover and we loved every minute of our lives together. I was also
classed as her lackey, and she could push me around at home any
which way … I just loved it, every bit of it.

SCENE 131 EXT. ROYAL BRISBANE HOSPITAL. DUSK.

*Traffic flashes by the Royal Brisbane Hospital, shot at three frames per second and
step printed. The movement of traffic is reflected in the shiny marble wall of the
hospital.*

SCENE 132 INT. A WARD – ROYAL BRISBANE HOSPITAL. DUSK.

*From the point of view of a person lying on a bed for radium treatment. The radium
machine spins around at head level.*

SCENE 133 INT. THE X-RAY ROOM – ROYAL BRISBANE HOSPITAL. DUSK.

On a fluoroscope a living X-ray of a man's throat makes swallowing movements.

TREVOR: [*voice over*] Four weeks later I received a call from Bonita. Koiki had been rushed to Brisbane for radium treatment. The cancer was spreading rapidly. Tragically, the case was still before the High Court. Phone calls were made to his lawyers: they too were impatient, but there was nothing they could do.

SCENE 134 INT. THE WARD – ROYAL BRISBANE HOSPITAL. DUSK.

An oxygen pump.

BONITA: [*voice over*] He was on oxygen all the time, and he'd say to me 'Turn the oxygen up.' And they'd say 'No, you can't have any more. It would only make you more sick.' And he'd just shake his head.

> *From the bed's point of view the curtain is pulled anonymously around, shot three frames per second and step printed.*

He'd ask me the time and I'd tell him 'Nine o'cock'. Dead on eleven o'clock he'd ask me the time again; you'd swear he was counting the minutes. He started gasping for breath. Then he died in my arms.

SCENE 135 MONTAGE.

Photographs of Koiki dissolving backwards through the decades of his life to the earliest photo of him standing on the beach at Las. Dissolve to:

A swimming shark, a Torres Strait pigeon and the sea raging against the reef at Las.

SCENE 136 EXT. TOWNSVILLE CEMETERY. DAY.

A white cross is hammered into the ground at the end of a freshly dug grave. The cross bears the inscription, 'In Loving Memory of Edward Koiki Mabo, 29-6-36 TO 21-1-92'. Bunches of flowers are pushed into the mound of earth, totally covering the grave.

TREVOR: [*voice over*] Koiki had decided a long time before his death that he wished to be buried on Murray Island. He'd chosen a special burial place on his ancestral land and had informed his family and close Islander friends.

> *Some time has passed. Bonita places flowers onto the grave.*

Despite Koiki's wish, Bonita and the family decided they wanted him to stay close by them, in Townsville.

> *Koiki's grave is seen in relation to other islander graves. Many of them have simple wooden crosses.*

In Island custom the grave of a loved one is left simple, almost like a pauper's grave, for several years. A special ceremony is then held: a tombstone opening to celebrate the life of the deceased.

> *The view across the Townsville cemetery.*

SCENE 137 BLACK.

A handwritten title card: 'Four months and ten days later ...'

SCENE 138 EXT. BONDI BEACH – SYDNEY. LATE AFTERNOON.

A Qantas plane flies across the sky in the late afternoon sun. A surfer catches a wave. Roller bladers take in the sun. A few strollers and joggers run along the beach.

TREVOR: [*voice over*] At the end of May I was in Sydney working on another film project when I received a call from Eddie Mabo Jnr: 'We're on our way to Canberra. The judgement's coming down on June third. The word is, it's looking good!'

SCENE 139 MONTAGE.

Points of view from inside a car cruising down the highway from Townsville. Time passes: late afternoon, dusk, night. Headlights beam down the road, through different landscapes and cities. Brisbane, Story Bridge and approaches to Sydney. Cars and trucks pass the 'Mabo' car.

Music: Sunrize Band, 'Land Rights'.

BONITA: [*voice over*] They rang and told us on Monday that the verdict was coming down on Wednesday. And I really wanted to be there, for that one especially. I went with Koiki to some of the cases when the court was on, and now he's not here for this one, I wanted to be there.

EDDIE JNR: [*voice over*] We didn't have that much time to think about it.

Mum said to Mal, let's go. It's two days. She just jumped in the car, we had twenty-four hours or something to get there.

Point of view from the car as it drives across the Sydney Harbour Bridge and out along Parramatta Road, through the suburbs of Sydney.

TREVOR: [*voice over*] And so it was that, when the High Court decision was handed down at one p.m. on June third, 1992, the Mabo family was at a Parramatta shopping complex, four hours from Canberra. They'd run out of time.

SCENE 140 EXT. PARRAMATTA SHOPPING TOWN. DAY.

Inside the mall, burger bars and shops.

TREVOR: [*voice over*] I drove to Parramatta and found the Mabo gang in a burger bar. Far from dispirited, their heads were in the clouds: they'd won. The High Court had ruled in favour of Eddie Mabo and his fellow plaintiffs. I could hardly believe it.

SCENE 141 MONTAGE.

Photographs: the Mabos in a car park. Mario, Celuia, Bethel, Eddie and Bonita hold a placard proclaiming, 'WE WON – MABO VRS QUEENSLAND GOVERNMENT – WE WON'.

EDDIE JNR: [*voice over*] Mum made up a plaque and stuck it on the car: 'We Won – Mabo versus Queensland Government – We Won'.

TV and radio news headlines outline the Mabo case victory. My hand opens the cover of the 1992 High Court judgement. Dissolve to:

Text: key words and phrases.

TREVOR: [*voice over*] The High Court determined that pre-existing land rights or 'native title' had not been extinguished on Murray Island. 'The Meriam people', the High Court said, 'are entitled as against the whole world to possession, occupation, use and enjoyment of the lands of the Murray Islands.' More than two hundred years of denial of indigenous land rights had collapsed. The land grab was over.

Bonita Mabo, Eddie Jnr and Celuia with their victory banner

SCENE 142 INT. NOEL PEARSON'S LAW OFFICE – MELBOURNE. DAY.

Noel Pearson in his office.

NOEL: The High Court could have said, 'This is about Murray Island', they could have quarantined it to the Torres Strait. The critical thing is they said, 'No it applies to the whole of Australia, let's establish the basic principles'. The High Court didn't create native title in nineteen ninety-two, the High Court said native title has always been there; its just that Australian law didn't recognise it before the third of June, nineteen ninety-two.

SCENE 143 INT. JUSTICE MOYNIHAN'S OFFICE – THE SUPREME COURT OF QUEENSLAND. DAY.

Justice Moynihan in his office.

JUSTICE MOYNIHAN: If you look at it in the specific context of Murray Island, I made findings about the sort of society they had, the relationship it had with the land and so on, and if you applied the doctrine of *terra nullius*, it said that that wasn't there, that didn't happen. That to me is an injustice. To say that we're going to pretend you're not here and that you haven't been here and established the sort of society and so on that you have established: if that of itself is not an injustice, then it provides a point of departure from which you can rapidly progress to injustice.

SCENE 144 INT. COURT NUMBER ONE – THE HIGH COURT OF AUSTRALIA. DAY.

The honourable justices file out of court.

HENRY: [*voice over*] To a person confronting it, it must have seemed a very radical thing for the High Court to do. But it was radical because the Australian situation was radical. They simply have joined the British Empire Common Law tradition. It's been there for a long time. And similar laws have existed in Spanish and Portuguese colonial empires. Australia was the anomalous one. It came as a shock to Australians because they had not been aware of just how out of step Australia was.

SCENE 145 EXT. THE HIGH COURT OF AUSTRALIA – CANBERRA. DAY.

Bryan Keon-Cohen stands outside, brief case in hand.

BRYAN: In the final analysis Eddie Mabo was reintroduced into the picture. The view the High Court took of it in their judgements was that those detailed findings by Mr Justice Moynihan of which people on Murray Island held rights and interests in land were irrelevant. They decided that all they needed to address was whether a native title had survived on Murray Island. The precise details of who had what right or interest in what block of land were matters for the community to work out in accordance with their own traditions and customs. So Eddie Mabo's widow, Bonita, and his children and grandchildren now enjoy native title and had Eddie Mabo lived, he too would have enjoyed those rights.

SCENE 146 MONTAGE.

TV news footage of the 1992 Australian Human Rights Award presentation. Photographs of Bonita Mabo and her daughter Malita in Sydney, with Labour Prime Minister Paul Keating.

TREVOR: [*voice over*] Later in nineteen ninety-two Eddie Mabo was posthumously awarded the Human Rights Medal, along with his fellow Islander plaintiffs. In January nineteen ninety-three the Australian newspaper declared him Australian of the Year. Later that year the Keating Government responded to the Mabo case by introducing native title legislation into the Federal Parliament.

> *TV news and radio regarding native title. State Premiers Jeff Kennett and Richard Court, Oppositon Leader John Hewson, businessman Hugh Morgan and parliamentarian John Stone, all condemn the High Court and the Keating Government's native title Act.*

STONE: ... Judicially, it's a disgrace; no one can argue that seven judges sitting on the bench have the power to so radically change the laws of this country ...

MORGAN: ... The naive adventurism of the High Court, the economic and social future of Australia has been put at risk, our territorial integrity …

SCENE 147 EXT. THE HIGH COURT OF AUSTRALIA – CANBERRA. DAY.

BRYAN: The debate surrounding native title I consider to have revealed an appalling racism and ignorance and prejudice amongst many high ranking politicians and bureaucrats and industry leaders and journalists who should have known a lot better. Politicians like Jeff Kennett saying that our suburban backyards were at risk. Aboriginals were supposed to be able to claim suburban backyards. Absolute nonsense, patent nonsense under the Mabo judgement and the Native Title Act. A real tragedy following Mabo was that the country was unable to elevate themselves with the High Court, into a new level of debate. To set aside past prejudices. They were only led to understand the crises, economic and social and political crises, that some politicians suggested were triggered by Mabo. Now that was a failure of national leadership of a profound nature.

SCENE 148 INT. THE LOUNGE ROOM – THE MABO RESIDENCE. DAY.

The house is full of activity. The TV news is on and Western Australian Premier, Richard Court, is mouthing off about native title, but everyone is ignoring him.

SCENE 149 EXT. THE BACKYARD – THE MABO RESIDENCE. DAY.

The family are having a barbeque. Eddie Jnr, Celuia, Bonita, Bethel, Malita, Murio and the extended family are there. There's zillions of grandchildren running around. Noel Loos is there too, having a beer and a quiet chat, sharing some stories. The subject of the court case comes up in conversation as everyone parties on.

MALITA: [*with a cheeky grin*] I never took any notice, like any interest, in things like that. I was too busy. I was too anxious to get dressed and go out. So I didn't have any interest in it. But I wouldn't ever say that to Dad. Even like now, doesn't worry me. I mean it's good that he did this thing but, oh shit, it has to come to an end sometime. Don't you just get sick of it dragging on? Like this filming. Oh I do. I just get sick of it. Mum just likes to see herself on TV.

We, the film crew, are part of the fun.

TREVOR: [*voice over*] Over the following years I maintained a close contact with the Mabo family. They showed me a warmth and a homeliness that I found easy to accept. They took me into their lives and have come to regard me as part of their family. The more time we spent together the clearer it became. I was no longer an observer in this story; I'd crossed the line.

SCENE 150 EXT. BONDI BEACH – SYDNEY. DUSK.

Dusk views along the beach. On the southern headland lights are on in the flats and apartments.

SCENE 151 INT. MY FLAT – BONDI. NIGHT.

Inside my flat the TV news is on in the corner; something about Century Zinc mine or the Wik Case. Noel Pearson gives a brief news bite on native title.

TREVOR: [*voice over*] One day I received a 'phone call from Bonita: they were planning Koiki's tombstone unveiling. 'Will you come and film it?' she asked. 'We want you to. We want it properly done and we want Big John' (my cameraman) 'to film it!'

SCENE 152 BLACK.

Handwritten title card: 'June 1995'.

SCENE 153 EXT. TOWNSVILLE CEMETERY. DAY.

A view across the breadth of the Townsville cemetery. At one side of the cemetery is Koiki's grave. Young Eddie is polishing the newly erected headstone made of shiny black marble. The wording on the tombstone is in gold lettering and in the middle is a bronze bust of Koiki smiling (or 'shining' as Henry Reynolds described him). Etched into the marble is a shark and a Torres Strait pigeon. Bonita, Malita and Celuia watch Eddie polish.

TREVOR: [*voice over*] In island custom a tombstone unveiling marks the end of the mourning period. The family is released from its grief by celebrating the life of the deceased loved one. The Mabos had spent the past twelve months planning and saving for the event. Guests were invited from around Australia.

Bonita Mabo and family beside the freshly polished tombstone of Koiki Mabo, June, 1995.

After the marble is cleaned the family pose for me, so I can take a photograph. Then Bonita and Malita patiently wrap the tombstone in brightly coloured floral material.

[*Sync*] Why are you wrapping up the tombstone?

MALITA: I don't know; don't ask me. Mum, why are we wrapping it up?

CELUIA: That's why they call it an unveiling!

EDDIE JNR: Tradition dictates that the tombstone is wrapped. The material represents a gift back to the community; in our culture, material is precious. They also like to keep the tombstone a big surprise. The tombstone ceremony is the way a grieving family can give back gifts to the community which supported them throughout their mourning.

At the graveside Eddie Jnr is wearing his 'cool' wrap-around sunglasses.

EDDIE JNR: It's been three years since Dad died, and tomorrow is June third, the anniversary of the High Court judgement, and that's why we chose this date for the tombstone opening. Grieving is now finished; the family is released from grieving.

George Kudub, Meb and Addie Salee finish the graveside preparations. They build a fence around the grave and lovingly tie decorations of dried grass around it. The headstone is further wrapped in more colourful layers of material. A woven mat is placed on the grave and gifts from large carry bags are placed on top of the mat. Woven island baskets are placed on the ground, yams, bananas and sweet potatoes are placed on top of the grave.

SCENE 154 EXT. THE SUBURBS – TOWNSVILLE. DAY.

In a paddock on the outskirts of the suburbs a small army of Islander men butchers a dozen pigs. There's a lot of laughter and joking as the pinkish flesh is cut into chunks and wrapped in coconut leaves. In the midst of the food preparations Eddie Jnr is interviewed by ABC Radio Melbourne, via a mobile phone. They question him about the customary practice of tombstone openings. Eddie explains that his father is buried in Townsville and tombstone unveilings are practiced on the mainland, wherever there are Islander populations.

ABC REPORTER: How many people do you expect to attend the ceremony?

EDDIE JNR: Well I don't think there's too many people left on Murray

Island right now! With the celebrations, the tradition on Murray is, we race with our dancing, to see who's gonna be the best dancers, so the competition is going to be thick and fast on Saturday night. You're missing out on a good thing!

A dozen fires, each piled with rocks, flares across the open paddock.

ABC REPORTER: Anita Keating and Robert Tickner are coming to the unveiling?

EDDIE JNR: They represent the wider Australian community paying their respects to my father and his achievements, and I'm thankful for that acknowledgment.

Once the flames have died the hot rocks are loaded with parcels of pork. More hot rocks are placed on top of the meat and the ground oven covered with sand.

SCENE 155 EXT. A HOUSE – MUNDINGBURRA. DAY.

That evening in Mundingburra, another suburb of Townsville, yet more food is prepared. Kumara is being chopped to make sop sop. As soon as the camera appears the women begin to sing and their children dance. Peak hour traffic flashes past this very suburban house on Ross River Road.

SCENE 156 EXT. TOWNSVILLE CEMETERY. DAY.

A huge crowd of family, friends, colleagues, local politicians, unionists and academics, both black and white, gather at the cemetery for the tombstone opening. The wife of the Australian Prime Minister Anita Keating, Chairperson of ATSIC Lois O'Donoghue and Aboriginal Affairs Minister Robert Tickner are greeted on their arrival by Bonita Mabo and Eddie Jnr. The media pack pounces upon them. Cameras are poked in their faces, conversations eavesdropped upon. A handful of Bonita's grandchildren are introduced to Mrs. Keating.

The ceremony commences with an old Meriam hymn sung by three hundred Murray Islanders. At the graveside, Bonita and Anita Keating stand solemnly together. A ribbon is cut, opening the entrance to the graveside, and Eddie's aunties and uncles, Bonita and Mrs Keating enter to witness the unveiling. Another Meriam hymn is sung and the layers of cloth are slowly peeled by Eddie's relatives, to reveal the shiny black marble. There's hardly a dry eye as the smiling bronze face of Eddie Mabo is revealed for the first time. Mrs Keating and Bonita are reflected in the marble tombstone. A preacher gives a graveside speech.

Bonita Mabo standing alongside Mrs. Annita Keating at the tombstone unveiling ceremony, Townsville, 3 June 1995.

PREACHER: Uncle Koiki used to come and sit with me and say, 'We've got to free our people from injustice and the policies that keep our people down'. He fought the government; he wanted the government to recognise his boundaries, that the land belonged to him. Now, today, people are jumping on the bandwagon of native title, they're proud of native title, but that all comes from this one man lying here.

Donald Whaleboat speaks to the throng from beside the grave.

DONALD: This is the official end of mourning, the official end of mourning when 'sorry' is finished. We can rejoice now because we know his spirit rests in peace, but is also still here with us. We carry that spirit that Koiki has given to us forever. When the unveiling of the headstone takes place, that also means the partner is also free, it is to say there is no more tears now.

The ceremony is concluded with another hymn. Multitudes of onlookers stand at the grave and photograph the headstone. They touch, stroke and admire it. Bryan Keon-Cohen takes some snaps. Noel Loos stares at the bust of Koiki, as if remembering his friend.

To one side of Koiki's grave a Channel Ten reporter brushes her hair back and does a 'stand-up' to camera. She has trouble saying 'tombstone' in her report and has to have several goes at it. Finally she shakes her head and asks her cameraman:

SECOND REPORTER: Is there another word for 'tombstone'?

SCENE 157 INT. THE YMCA STADIUM – TOWNSVILLE. DAY.

Trestle tables are laid out in the centre of the stadium. On the table are bowls of turtle meat, chicken, pork, sop sop, rice, damper, cakes and fried scones.

TREVOR: [*voice over*] That night there was an open invitation to the traditional feast and dancing that completes a tombstone opening.

There is a huge crowd of people surrounding the tables and digging into the food, both Islanders and Europeans.

After the feast the modern stadium is transformed by traditional Murray Island dancing and singing. The air is full of whoops and ear splitting whistles. The stamping of the dancers grows heavier and the leaps lighter as the celebration continues into the night.

The dancing is dramatically intercut with close-ups of the tombstone as if lit by moonlight. Koiki's bronze smiling face and close-ups of text on the tombstone – 'Born 1936', 'Mabo case', 'Died 1992', 'In Loving Memory' – are intercut with foot stomps, leaps in the air, Gail Mabo dancing and Bonita sprinkling talcum powder on the backs of dancers.

SCENE 158 EXT. TOWNSVILLE. NIGHT.

From Castle Hill a view of Townsville and the lights of suburbia.

SCENE 159 EXT. TOWNSVILLE CEMETERY. NIGHT.

A night view across the cemetery.

SCENE 160 EXT. TOWNSVILLE CEMETERY. EARLY MORNING.

A bright red swastika has been sprayed onto Koiki's tombstone. Bonita stands in front of the headstone, traumatised. Celuia wipes tears from her eyes. The local police wander through the cemetery. A policeman fingerprints the tombstone. Islander and European friends surround the vandalised grave in silent disbelief. The word 'ABO' has also been sprayed on the side of the grave.

Alec Illin, a Townsville Aborigine, wraps his huge arms around Bonita and rages at the sight of the desecration.

ALEC: We're doing things here to try and create harmony and respect and this is what we have to put up with. This city should be ashamed of the people that live in it. There's no further reconciliation in this city, nothing will ever be reconciled … for a champion such as this; he's been a champion in this community all his life and this is what they do. They've got no guts; they take advantage of the darkness of the night to come down here and do this.

> *Local news crews arrive. They too are completely shattered by the nastiness of the attack. A white friend of the family looks at the grave, Celuia Mabo standing next to him.*

FRIEND: This is very sad.
CELUIA: It sucks, really!

> *Bonita, in a fragile state, struggles through several TV news interviews. A*

young female journalist from WIN TV points her mike at Bonita and asks her to count so she can check her sound level.

THIRD REPORTER: Okay, the grave looked so lovely yesterday and now this, today. How does it make you feel?

BONITA: Sick to the stomach. Everything went over so beautiful yesterday and to wake up to this is a nightmare.

THIRD REPORTER: Your husband was a very prominent person: has anything like this happened before?

BONITA: No, nothing like this.

THIRD REPORTER: Okay, how would you describe the people who are responsible for this?

BONITA: They're just a low down mob of racist bastards!

THIRD REPORTER: Okay, that's good!

Henry Reynolds and Noel Loos comfort Bonita at the grave.

BONITA: Once I put the headstone down, all my mourning time would be over. It means the end of grieving time for me and my children and that I can get on with my life. And now its just starting again … like waking up to a big nightmare.

Mario Mabo has a conversation with a group of island men as they examine the tombstone.

MARIO: This sort of thing never used to happen in Australia, only in America; but now it's come here too. We've decided to take him back to Murray Island; we've already talked.

Margaret Reynolds comforts one of Bonita's grandchildren at the grave when he asks her a question.

GRANDSON: What does 'Abo' mean?

MARGARET: It doesn't mean anything; it's just a bad word.

Margaret Reynolds is interviewed at the cemetery. In the background is Koiki's desecrated grave.

We knew Eddie from the best part of thirty years … It's really hard to believe … It's a very sad day for Australia when a national hero for the indigenous community, and indeed for many fair-minded Australians, would – we see this desecration … Um …

She pauses and wipes tears from her eyes.

Bonita Mabo and daughter Celuia inspect the vandalised tombstone, Townsville, June, 1995.

Well, I suppose what is distressing is that it's clearly been organised. The spiritual impact for the family is – It can't be calculated. But from a social-cohesion point of view, which is the way I look at it, it is very concerning that there is this element out there in the Australian community and in this part of the world where reconciliation and understanding, all that Eddie meant, is just so important for the future of good race relations. The High Court decision has been flashed around the world as indicative of Australia ending so much negativity in relation to indigenous people. And the desecration of the tombstone is a very damaging message that's going to go around the world too.

SCENE 161 INT. THE POLICE STATION – TOWNSVILLE. DAY.

At a local press conference an officer is interviewed by journalists.

FOURTH REPORTER: There's some talk of right-wing extremists being involved in this; is that your view?

OFFICER: That would only be supposition, because nobody knows who is responsible for this or whether there are any racial or political overtones at all. It's all supposition at this stage and the police are dealing with it with an open mind. It may simply be a case of wilful damage of a tombstone and it may be juveniles involved. People should remain calm, I would be very concerned if this evolved into clashes on the streets of Townsville.

FOURTH REPORTER: Is there any indication at that this stage that it could be somebody of extreme views, or just kids and juveniles?

OFFICER: The nature of the offence doesn't indicate that it's any particular person at all. It could be white adults involved, it could be Aboriginal or Islander juveniles involved. We don't know! I think it's been blown out of proportion.

SCENE 162 EXT. TOWNSVILLE CEMETERY. DAY.

The tombstone is carefully removed from the grave by a stone mason, with the aid of some strong Island men. By this stage a large crowd has gathered. There is an air of stunned disbelief as the truck drives off with the marble headstone.

Audio: radio and TV news and current affairs. A montage of voices about the tombstone desecration. The feeling is outrage, much of the discussion is about racism in North Queensland. One caller thinks Eddie Mabo is Australia's Martin Luther King, another says Eddie Mabo was a very powerful black man, and that's threatening. Voices from Federal Parliament are heard: Keating and Howard express their condolences to the Mabo family. Keating offers financial support to relocate the grave.

Eddie Jnr sits beside his father's desecrated grave, without the headstone.

EDDIE JNR: We wanted to make the tombstone unveiling an inclusive ceremony, because human rights and the legal challenges my father fought for belonged to everyone. We wanted this to be a monument for all Australia; we wanted it to be accessible for everyone. But now no one can guarantee that this won't happen again, and it's reinforced within the family that Dad would be safer on Murray Island. I think if Dad could communicate with us now he'd probably say, 'Take me back to Mer!' He'd say, 'Bury me at Las!', being Dad's birthplace. He would say, 'Wow, even in death I hold the attention of Australia!'

SCENE 163 BLACK.

Handwritten title card: 'Three months later ...'

SCENE 164 EXT. TOWNSVILLE CEMETERY. EARLY MORNING.

At first light a hessian curtain is erected around Koiki's grave. Grave diggers slowly commence digging. They whistle, sing and light-heartedly joke with each other as they dig spade after spade of earth.

The plastic liner of the coffin containing Koiki's remains is lifted out of the grave by four undertakers, placed inside a new casket, and sealed.

The coffin is placed in the rear of a hearse and driven out of the cemetery.

TREVOR: [*voice over*] On September Twelfth, Koiki's remains were exhumed. The Federal Government had came good with an offer of financial assistance for the family to relocate the grave. Nothing had come of the police investigation. Three months after the desecration the police were still denying the existence of right-wing groups in Townsville.

SCENE 165 EXT. THE AIRSTRIP – MURRAY ISLAND. DAY.

Koiki's coffin is carried across the Murray Island airstrip.

SCENE 166 EXT. A JUNGLE TRACK – MURRAY ISLAND. DAY.

The casket is handed over several times to different pallbearers as the mourning party descends through rainforest and clearings of tall creaking bamboo. Bonita and some other members of the mourning party are sobbing.

SCENE 167 EXT. LAS VILLAGE – MURRAY ISLAND. DAY.

The coffin is carried through the village at Las and placed in an open bamboo-and-palm-leaf shelter erected under a tree. Young and old Murray Islanders stand quietly together around the coffin. Some wipe tears from their eyes. Only the sound of the raging reef breaks the silence. Bonita leans on the lid of the coffin and wails.

A dog sits in front of the bamboo fence on the beach and stares out to sea. The water is turbulent and windy, the tide surges into the shore line. A young boy spears sardines on the reef. A dingy full of people races across the horizon line.

Eddie Jnr. stands next to his father's coffin, which has been draped with a Torres Strait flag.

EDDIE JNR: Dad before he died said he wanted to be buried at Sagir, on his own land. When we lost him it was really hard for Mum to let go, with the grieving process. From my point of view it seemed like Dad had so much foresight it was unreal, given that he said he wanted to be buried here, away from mainland Australia, away from any enemies he may have … Then having that happen on June third …

He laughs.

'Well, there you go, guys, time to move!' The significance of the place we're going to bury him is that his ancestors are not far from his final resting place. The ten-year battle with the land claim was for this place: he's secured it for the family, myself, generations to come, to enjoy, so why not have our hero on site with us?

SCENE 168 EXT. LAS VILLAGE – MURRAY ISLAND. DAWN.

In the half-light of dawn the coffin is barely visible beneath a blue plastic tarp. Light rain is falling.

By lantern light Islander relatives, together with the Mabo family, sit around the coffin for their final hours of mourning. Jack Wailu, Eddie Jnr and George Kudub sit next to each other.

SCENE 169 EXT. LAS VILLAGE – MURRAY ISLAND. DAY.

Later that morning the coffin is picked up by warrior pallbearers and carried through Las village.

SCENE 170 EXT. A JUNGLE TRACK – MURRAY ISLAND. DAY.

A procession of singing Islanders follows the casket along a jungle path.

SCENE 171 EXT. THE GRAVESITE – MURRAY ISLAND. DAY.

They rest the coffin on bamboo poles above the concrete vault. The Mabo family and mourners surround the grave, singing. The headstone is covered, wrapped in material. Bonita wipes tears from her eyes, her grandson next to her erupts into tears. Other Murray Island children are crying.

The coffin is lowered into the vault.

Sam Wailu conducts the service.

SAM: We now commit body of uncle bilong me, friend bilong mi fella, father, to the ground.

> *Later, a TV reporter stands behind the headstone doing a stand-up to camera. Islanders stand around watching her with amusement.*

FIFTH REPORTER: Tomorrow the headstone will be unveiled. Islanders … Sorry … Tomorrow, the tombstone will be unveiled. Islanders will perform a traditional dance for Eddie Mabo, marking his place among the Meriam people as a spiritual leader.

CAMERAMAN: [*out of view*] Do another one.

SCENE 172 EXT. KOROG VILLAGE – MURRAY ISLAND. DAY.

James and Mary Rice sit in their village at Korog. James is speaking emotionally, wiping tears from his eyes.

JAMES: He's resting from his good work. I can picture him in my memories, of what we were doing in the court. I can picture him, but it's like too late for me to say that: he's in the graveyard. I'm really glad he's back on his island and buried in his place, in the area where he was a little boy growing up. He's one of the Meriam, a Murray Islander. His memorial here is on native-title land. We'll hold fast in the native title. We don't want to lose it.

SCENE 173 EXT. THE GRAVESITE – MURRAY ISLAND. DAY.

A single piece of cloth is removed to reveal the headstone. I take a photograph of Bonita and Eddie Jnr standing next to the glistening black stone. Other Islanders take photographs of the headstone and wipe away tears. Bonita sits smiling at the edge of Koiki's grave. Behind her is Eddie's shining face and the engravings of his shark and pigeon totems.

BONITA: He got his wish … and I think that makes it easier for us to accept. The hardest part will be to go back to Townsville and leave him up here; but then again I suppose I have to let go. I've got no choice. [*Smiling*] But I do feel at ease that he's here.

> *Jack Wailu climbs into his wheelchair and is wheeled away from the gravesite.*

JACK: Our forefathers used to say, '*Ir kez bizar, sep bizar*'; it means, 'Follow the narrow path, the right path', '*sep bizar*'. It means Eddie has to go down in his own ground in his own property. There's no doubt about it. So, Eddie, welcome home, you're here with us.

SCENE 174 EXT. LAS VILLAGE – MURRAY ISLAND. NIGHT.

Murray Islanders have gathered at Las for a Malo ceremony in honour of Koiki Mabo. Jack Wailu sits in his wheelchair in the middle of a group of senior Murray Island men and women. He's playing a drum and singing solo a sacred Malo song. He struggles hard to sing loudly, forces it out with all his strength. His soft voice has immense passion and emotion.

Bonita Mabo and Eddie Jnr. beside Koiki Mabo's resurrected tombstone on Mer, September, 1995.

The Malo mask comes out of the darkness. The central dancer wears a turtle shell mask decorated with feathers. He dances slowly, to the beat of Jack's drum, stepping over young boy initiates laying prostrate on the ground.

TREVOR: [*voice over*] For many Australians the name 'Mabo' has become a symbol of hope. On a personal level I only briefly knew the man. But in making this film with his family I've come to learn that Koiki was flesh and blood like the rest of us: a husband, a father, an uncle and a friend.

SCENE 175 EXT. LAS VILLAGE – MURRAY ISLAND. DAY.

Waves break against the reef at Las. Koiki, wearing a red lava lava, wades in the shallow waters off the reef.

TREVOR: [*voice* over] His struggle was for recognition, tolerance and acceptance. His vision went beyond the immediate needs of his own family, island and people: it was to bring the best of two cultures together.

KOIKI: [*voice* over] I think I've got about ninety-nine percent of winning the case. Personally, it means a victory for me. But that not only means a victory for me, it means victory for the Murray Islanders, the rest of Torres Strait Islands and of course the mainland of Australia, the indigenous people, our Aboriginal brothers and sisters: it also means a victory for them as well. And of course it will also mean that the European law at last is in a position to recognise the traditional customs, customary laws and practises in this country, and that multi-culturalism would be meaningful. And I think that's what Australia should be all about.

Audio: Jack Wailu's singing continues.

Mabo stands out on the reef alone, a tiny speck against the sea and sky.

THE END

THE POST-PRODUCTION SCRIPT

Mr. Kaba Noah with "Wasikor" the sacred drum of Malo, the octopus god

Black. Fade up: 'Film Australia presents'. Fade to Black. Fade up a wide shot aerial of islands. Dissolve to: a wide tracking shot of mountain and sea. A school of fish. Wide-shot pan of seagulls flying over water. Time-lapse of a fence on a beach as clouds and clouds.

Mid shot of a man swinging a child. Mid shot jump cut of the man and child. Wide shot tilt over the ocean to the horizon, and sky.

TREVOR: [*voice over*] This is the story of a small island and an extraordinary man. The man was born on the island, but lived most of his life in exile.

> *Dissolve to: a medium-wide shot following four men carrying a coffin. Dissolve to: a medium-wide shot of traditionally dressed men approaching with the coffin.*

[*Voice over*] ... His greatest victory was won only after his death – and only after his death did the island wholeheartedly welcome him home.

> *Zoom out from the hat of a woman crying over the coffin to a medium-wide shot of the coffin under a canopy. Zoom out from a close-up of a mask to a medium-wide shot of two dancers. Tilt down from a close-up of the bust on the gravestone to the engraved words: 'In loving memory of Edward Koiki Mabo, Born Murray Island 29-6-1936, Died 21-1-1992 Aged 56 years'.*

[*Voice over*] ... By then, the island and the man, between them, had changed the face of Australia. Very few of us know much about the man, though his name is a household word. The islanders called him Koiki. The world knew him as Eddie Mabo.

> *Medium close-up: the smiling face of Eddie Koiki. Cut to black.*

> *Title: 'MABO'. Fade up the rest of title: 'Life of an Island Man'.*

> *A medium-wide shot of Eddie Koiki Mabo walking on the beach with his spear pans to mid shot.*

[*Voice over*] In 1989, I made a film with Eddie Koiki. His name was not yet famous. But he was already seven years into the defining battle of his life: to have the High Court of Australia recognise that he and his people were the rightful owners of Murray Island in the Torres Strait.

> *Close-up of Koiki.*

KOIKI: According to my tradition, those fish, the prawn, whatever is in that sea belongs to me and my people. That is important. And that of course ought to be claimed that I'm claiming in the High Court.

Wide tracking shots along a road from a car: houses, various stretches of road, shops.

TREVOR: [*voice over*] It's one of the ironies of Eddie's life that he lived most of it in the suburbs of Townsville, a far cry from the reefs and islands of the Torres Strait.

Tea pours into a cup. Pan out to a medium-wide shot of two women, Trevor, and baby to mid shot of a woman and baby. Fade out music.

[*Out of view*] Who wants tea?

BONITA: [*out of view*] Yes please.

Mid shot of a boy holding a puppy.

TREVOR: [*voice over*] Since Eddie's death, I've become close to his wife Bonita and her family. Netta still lives in the Townsville family home that she and Eddie bought together … still devotes most of her time and energy to the family they raised.

Close-up of Bonita picking up the baby, who reaches for the microphone. Pan in to extreme close-up of baby's face.

BONITA: [*out of view*] You get it.

Hands pass over the barbecue. Mid shot of a woman. Medium-wide shot of the kids at the table. Pan up to a mid shot of a person in a blue shirt.

TREVOR: [*voice over*] It was the family's idea, as much as mine, to make another film about Eddie Mabo, about the human being they loved, the legal battler, husband, father, neighbour and friend.

Mid shot of two men at the table. Close-up as a dish passes a man's face. Pan out to mid shot of a man and girl. Wide shot of the group, two tables and barbecue. Mid shot woman and man holding a dog. Super: 'CATH & GEORGE CARTER, Neighbours'

[*Out of view*] So how long have you lived next door to each other?

GEORGE CARTER: I've been here thirty-four …

CATH CARTER: Thirty years. Terrible neighbours.

Pan right to Bonita, holding the dog, laughing.

BONITA: They don't want to get rid of me.

GEORGE CARTER: [*voice over*] And I don't think we've ever had a cross word, you know that? Never.

Medium-wide shot of George Carter with dog and Cath.

CATH CARTER: Never. We haven't had a cross word with any of our neighbours.

The dog growls. Laughter.

GEORGE CARTER: He don't like these fellows.

CATH CARTER: He's got something in his hands, see?

GEORGE CARTER: Yeah, yeah.

TREVOR: [*out of view*] So what sort of things did you used to see Eddie doing around here?

Medium-wide shot of Cath and George with the dog and Bonita in the corner of the frame.

GEORGE CARTER: Around here? Oh, he used to do a lot of things.

CATH CARTER: When he done that school.

GEORGE CARTER: He was on that boat, more than anything else, wasn't he? Eh? In the boat.

Tilt up a photo of Koiki.

CATH CARTER: [*voice over*] That's right.

GEORGE CARTER: [*voice over*] Yeah. I don't know how many coats of paint he put on that boat … I know when old Eddie went, oh, we lost a good friend you know.

Mid shot Cath and George with dog. The dog growls.

[*To the dog*] Oh, shut up.

Mid shot of Gail Mabo and her daughter. Super: 'GAIL MABO, Daughter'.

GAIL MABO: He was determined from the first time he said, he was fighting for land rights. We all thought he was joking. We kept calling him, 'Oh, Dad, you're a radical', you know. 'When you're gone, you'll have to wear the colours and all.'

Pan across a photo: barristers and Koiki.

[*Voice over*] But he was determined; he said he was doing it, and he did it. He set his mind to it.

MARGARET REYNOLDS: [*voice over*] Well, he was an intensely political person.

Mid shot of Margaret Reynolds. Super: 'MARGARET REYNOLDS, Friend'. Close-up.

Everything he said and did seemed to have a political motivation. I mean you only had to meet him and in the first few minutes of conversation he would be telling you about something that had to be done. He was not going to sit back and let the world continue as many of his countrymen did.

A hand writes. Extreme close-up: lips smoking. Zoom out to a close-up of Koiki. Music and singing. A shaky extreme close-up of the hand writing. Zoom out to mid shot of Koiki. Pan right across open books and documents to a mid shot of a person turning pages. Dissolve through extreme close-ups of writing.

TREVOR: [*voice over*] He was not just a talker, but a writer too. He poured out a stream of words on paper: letters, diaries, speeches, manifestoes. Every draft of every document, public and private, was filed away for posterity. 'Some day', he would tell his friends, 'I'll be famous'.

Dissolve to extreme close-up tilt down the words of a letter manifesto.

KOIKI: 'To my people, the Torres Strait Islanders, the aim of this court case ...'

Dissolve to an extreme close-up pan across words. Tilt up over many papers and drawings ...

NOEL LOOS: [*voice over*] His own words and his private papers say that the two great loves of his life were his great love for his wife Netta – Bonita Koiki ...

Mid shot of Noel Loos. Super: 'NOEL LOOS, Friend & Biographer'.

[*Sync*] ... And the great love for Murray Island and even the people of Murray Island with whom he had a great turbulent relationship.

Black.

Intertitle: 'Piadaram Man'.

Tracking shot over water. Medium-wide archival shot of kids on a boat.

Archival mid-shot of the back of a child in the boat. Medium-wide archival shot of kids on the bow of the boat. Tracking shot over water. A wide tracking shot of the beach from the water. Wide shot: Murray Island from the air.

TREVOR: [*voice over*] Murray Island – which Eddie's people call 'Mer' – the Torres Strait.

Wide tracking shot of the shore line. Archival mid shot of men in a boat blowing shells. Sound effect: a horn. Wide shot tracking a motorboat across water. Fade music and singing. Wide shot of men on the beach building a bamboo fence. Sound effect: chopping. Wide shot of women on the beach building the bamboo fence. Close-up of Koiki at the bamboo fence.

[*Voice over*] Eddie Koiki Mabo was born and raised in the village of Las. It's the first place on the island to see the rising sun … and it bears the full brunt of the easterly winds that sweep in from the Coral Sea.

A mid shot of Eddie Mabo and Jack Wailu at the bamboo fence. Wide shot. Wide shot of a woman walking along the beach. Medium-wide shot of two boys in the water with a spear. Music stings. Pan with distant seagulls over the sea. Sound effect: seagulls call. A mid shot Eddie and Jack at the bamboo fence.

[*Voice over*] When I filmed with him back in nineteen eighty-nine, Koiki told me about his early life and the culture of Murray Island.

Medium-wide shot of the two men working on the bamboo fence. One is Koiki, the other Jack Wailu. Close-up of Jack's face.

KOIKI: [*voice over*] We are both Piadaram, clansman. We occupy this area of Las …

Mid shot of Koiki working on the wall.

[*Sync, indicating Jack*] … He lived there in his Las and I lived next door.

Wide shot of people carrying bamboo on the beach.

[*Voice over*] … And today we're doing exactly what our ancestors have done in the past to protect themselves from the Sagir wind, which is the trade wind.

Dissolve to: a black-and-white archival photo of the beach. A black-and-

white archival photo, a wide-shot of three people by a hut. A black-and-white photo, a wide-shot of large huts. Zoom in to an Islander standing by the hut. Dissolve to: a black-and-white archival photo of a stone club. Zoom out to reveal two men holding it.

[*Voice over*] All this area was, or inhabited by Piadaram people …

Close-up of Koiki.

[*Sync*] … From my grandfather to my father and myself, makes it up to twenty generations altogether that we've occupied this area.

A black-and-white photo, a medium-wide-shot of a young Koiki and Jack Wailu. Zoom in to Eddie on the left. A wide shot of Eddie and Jack walking along the beach.

JACK WAILU: [*voice over, subtitled*] I remember, way back when we were kids, our grandfathers and fathers …

Mid shot of Jack. Super: 'JACK WAILU, Neighbour'.

[*Sync, subtitled*]… They'd sing out to us to come and sit with them on the bamboo fence along the beach and they'd talk to us about our traditional culture. And we used to take heed, me and Eddie.

Wide shot of the beach. Pan right. Medium-wide shot of two men chopping in the forest. Music and singing. Close-up of a man. Tilt down to his spade digging the ground. Mid shot of Jack Wailu.

[*Subtitled*] Our grandfathers and father used to tell us the dates and months to plant our gardens: all our bananas, pumpkins and watermelons.

Mid shot of a woman digging. Pan right to a little girl, also digging. Hands pull yams from the ground. Zoom out to mid shot.

Black-and-white archival medium-wide shot of women carrying plants. Close-up of a woman in the bamboo. Mid shot of the woman's back. Mid shot of the woman chopping. Close-up.

Black-and-white archival wide shot of a person climbing a tree. Medium-wide shot of a man chopping leaves. Medium-wide shot of three people cutting bamboo. Black-and-white archival wide shot of a traditional dance. Fade out music and singing out.

Mid shot of Jack and Koiki. Close-up of feet dancing. Music and Singing. Mid shot of two dancers in traditional dress. Medium-wide shot of the dancers. Mid shot of the two men sitting.

KOIKI: Most of our songs and stories are in dances, and tells mainly about what type of weather or natural event that happens on Murray Island: sometimes about catching sardines at a certain time of the year when sardines are plentiful, or it's the right time to catch them with a weiris – it's an implement that you see at the back of me. And they're still being practiced today.

Wide shot of dancers on the beach. Close-up of Jack Wailu with a headdress. Medium-wide shot of the dancers. Black-and-white archival wide shot of a man running into the water. Medium-wide shot of the dancers. Medium-wide shot of people playing instruments. Mid shot of the dancers. Pan right.

Black-and-white archival medium-wide shot of men with sardines. Extreme close-up of hands carving a stick. Close-up of the man, James Rice. Mid shot of the James and a woman. Music and singing fade out. Close-up of hands making a weiris. Tilt up to the James's face. Super: 'JAMES RICE, Cousin'. Medium-wide shot of James and the woman sitting. Close-up of James.

JAMES RICE: My mother is related to Koiki's mother, and I call Koiki my 'cousin brother'; 'real cousin, black cousin', I always say.

James' hands work away. Zoom out to a mid shot of James making a basket.

TREVOR: [*voice over*] Shortly after his birth, Koiki's mother died, and his natural father gave him up for adoption to his mother's brother, Benny Mabo, and his wife Maiga. By islander law, Benny Mabo became Koiki's father.

A close-up black-and-white photo of Koiki's adoptive father, Benny. Pan right to Maiga.. Mid shot of both. A mid shot black-and-white photo of four men. Zoom in to a close-up of Benny. Close up of James Rice.

JAMES RICE: Koiki was adopted, traditionally, because of Benny; Benny hasn't got a child. He was adopted by blood, you know, blood relation. He was adopted. That's why all the lands belong to him.

A black-and-white photo of Koiki's feet. Tilt up to his head and shoulders.

[*Voice over*] No one can interfere. So he can claim Mabo land.

TREVOR: [*voice over*] But the white man did not recognise islander law or title to land – and from eighteen seventy-nine, when Queensland annexed Murray Island, white rule was absolute.

A black-and-white archival wide shot of people marching along the beach. Music. Archival black-and-white mid shot of the Chief Protector. An archival wide shot of many children doing exercises. An extreme close-up of a child.

[*Voice over*] The Chief Protector of Aborigines had this film made in 1936, the year that Koiki was born.

A medium-wide shot of kids projected on a wall. A black-and-white archival wide shot of men walking between rows of children. A black-and-white archival wide shot of men standing with flags. A black-and-white archival wide shot of a white man standing over a group of seated black people. An extreme close-up of a black face. A black-and-white archival wide shot of a ceremony. A mid shot of the same ceremony.

[*Voice over*] Even though Murray Islanders could elect their own council, their leaders were subordinate to the protector's authority. Under Queensland law, he controlled every aspect of island life. He dictated wages. He authorised every journey between the islands.

A black-and-white archival shot of a distant island between two trees.. A black-and-white archival wide shot of a large group of Islanders. A black-and-white archival wide shot: rows of women and men approaching. A black-and-white archival wide shot: rows of girls and boys approaching.

[*Voice over*] Above all, he regulated the Islanders' private lives. Before marriage, the sexes were strictly separated. And they could only wed with his permission.

Dissolve to: a black-and-white wide shot archival photo of a wedding. Zoom in to the couple. Dissolve to: a medium-wide shot of the same photo. Pan across people to the wedding couple. A silhouette of trees against the sky. A wider shot: the silhouette of trees on a hill against the sky. Music fades out. Wind effect. Mid shot of a man and woman. Pan right, across the table to another man and woman. Medium close-up of Koiki and Bonita. Zoom out to mid shot.

[*Voice over*] As Eddie recalled for us one evening, the education he was given on the island was basic.

KOIKI: [*voice over*] My life was more of a semi-tribal situation where I didn't know a word of English until I was 14.

A medium-wide shot black-and-white archival photo of a teacher pointing to the blackboard on which is written, 'One King One Flag'. Zoom out to a wide shot of the group. A black-and-white archival wide shot of kids coming out of school.

TREVOR: [*voice over*] It was assumed that no islander child had the ability to progress beyond primary school. But there was one teacher, Robert Miles, whom young Koiki liked and admired.

A black-and-white photo, close-up of Robert Miles. Zoom in to extreme close-up.

KOIKI: [*voice over*] He said, look, you'd better start digging your toes in and learn English, because one day you are going to go to the mainland and seek employment and you'll be confronted with millions who speak just English. I saw the magic and learned it.

Extreme close-up of Koiki's mouth and cigarette. Tilt up to the eyes. Music. A pen scratches on paper.

TREVOR: [*voice over*] Intelligence, determination, ambition: Koiki displayed all three from an early age. Now another trait emerged.

A black-and-white photo, a mid shot of Koiki as a young man. Zoom in to close-up. Music fades.

KOIKI: [*voice over*] At the age of sixteen I started to question the system, on Murray where I grew up: why Queensland treated my people the way they did. Why was it so? Were we different?

A black-and-white photo, mid shot of two men and guitars. Tilt up to close-up of the young Koiki, standing behind them.

NOEL LOOS: [*voice over*] When Koiki was sixteen he got into trouble with the Islander Council on Murray Island. He had a romance with some island girl, and this was seen as a crime by the Islander Court, which of course was implementing Queensland laws, and so he was then exiled from the island for a year; that was the sentence he got.

Track along the surface of the water. Music and singing. Archival black-and-white wide shot of a man on the bow of a sailboat. Close-up of Noel.

[*Sync*] This began a period of exile throughout his whole life, really.

A medium-wide shot pans with sailboats on the water.

[*Voice over*] He found himself until virtually he died in conflict with the Murray Island people and with the Queensland Government.

A wide shot of sailboats on water. A medium-wide shot of sailboats ploughing forward. Mid shot of men on the boat. Pan right to a wide shot of another boat.

TREVOR: [*voice over*] In exile, Koiki found work on the Torres Strait pearling fleets and immediately started to challenge the conditions set by the Queensland Government.

Medium-wide shot side of a boat. Mid shot of a man on the boat.

KOIKI: [*voice over*] Well, why was things like pearling industry operating in the Straits where the islanders were paid lower than the Malays and the Europeans?

Close-up of a man in diver's head gear. Medium-wide shot of a diver going under water. Medium-wide shot of the water surface. Medium-wide shot of men on the boat. Medium-wide shot four men on the boat. Wide shot of the side of the boat. Medium-wide shot of men on the boat.

TREVOR: [*voice over*] When his period of exile was over, Koiki decided not to return to Murray Island.

KOIKI: [*voice over*] I decided to come to the mainland to find why was my people treated the way they did. Why they weren't equal to the rest of Australians.

Wide shot of the side of the boat in full sail. Fade to black.

Fade up on an extreme wide shot of fields and hills. Wide shot of ploughed earth on a hill. Close-up of fire in a canefield.

TREVOR: [*voice over*] He jumped ship in Cairns and drifted into a series of labouring jobs – cutting cane, laying railways – the only kind of work available to Torres Strait Islanders in Australia in the nineteen fifties.

Dissolve to: a black-and-white photo, a mid shot of men working on railway tracks. Zoom out to medium-wide shot. Dissolve to: a close-up of burning cane. Tilt up the cane. Dissolve to: a black-and-white photo, wide shot of men working on railway tracks. Zoom in to a mid shot of one man. Dissolve to: a black-and-white photo, wide shot of men working on the tracks. Zoom in to mid shot of three men. Dissolve to: a wide shot burning cane. A black-and-white photo of a man's legs. Tilt up to mid shot. Fade out music and singing.

KOIKI: [*voice over*] When I first landed here I was like a total stranger or foreigner coming into Australia. To a complete strange world who speak strange languages and to be mixed up with strange people.

> *Wide shot roadside with moving campervans and cars. Mid shot of a woman coming out of a pool. Tilt up as she climbs, zoom in to close-up. Wide shot of a large group of bathers on the bow of a boat. Close-up of a woman smelling flowers. Medium-wide shot of a boy and puppy in front of a house.*

And from then on, I started learning a bit more about the white man and his way of life on the mainland.

> *A medium-wide shot of a young woman hosing a garden. Mid shot of two women and a boy at a table. Zoom in to close-up of the boy.*

WOMAN: Drink this, it's cold. Crystal, your turn.
CRYSTAL: No.
TREVOR: [*voice over*] And then, in a shanty town on the edge of a sugar plantation, he met Bonita, whose family had been brought to work the cane fields from distant Vanuatu.

> *Mid shot four people at a table. A black-and-white photo, medium-wide shot of young Koiki and Bonita. Zoom in to mid shot of the couple.*

[*Out of view*] Bonita, when is the first time that you met Koiki?

> *Mid shot Bonita and Celuia Mabo at a table.*

CELUIA: Eighteen hundred and …

> *Laughter. Close-up of Malita West, also at the table.*

BONITA: [*out of view*] Nineteen fifty-eight.

> *Mid shot Bonita and Malita.*

MALITA: [*out of view*] And it was love …
BONITA: … At first sight!
CELUIA: [*out of view*] Oh, sweet.

> *Close-up of Malita.*

TREVOR: [*out of view*] And when you met him, how old was he and how old were you?

> *Mid shot of Bonita and Celuia.*

CELUIA: Come on truthfully.

BONITA: Do I have to say?
CELUIA: Yes.
BONITA: I was young.
CELUIA: Yeah, how young is 'young'?
MALITA: [*out of view*] We're all big now, Mum, you can tell us.
BONITA: Yeah, I suppose.

> *A black-and-white photo, mid shot of two women with others behind them. Zoom in to close-up on the young Bonita.*

[*Voice over*] Well, I was seventeen, going on eighteen.

> *A black-and-white photo, mid shot of two men. Zoom in to close-up of the young Koiki.*

He was on the railway and he was working as a fettler on the fettler gang and he was out west.

> *A handwritten date on paper. Pan left to the words, 'To my darling …'*

KOIKI: [*voice over*] Fettler Gang, Jardine Valley, twenty-fourth of July, nineteen fifty-nine. To my darling: …

> *Extreme close-up of Bonita's face. Close-up of her hands holding the letter. Dissolve to: a black-and-white photo, close-up of young Koiki.*

[*Voice over*] … I think it's about time we should call each other 'darling' because we have known each other well enough and besides we are love for sure. Yes. P.S. We are in love, of course.

> *Close-up of Bonita's hands flipping the page of the letter.*

[*Voice over*] … The rising of the waves … just hang on to me. My love to you and the breeze on your lips are my kisses to you.

> *Extreme close-up Bonita's face. Medium-wide shot of Bonita at a table inside.*

[*Voice over*] And give my kind regard to your mum, please. I remain your most sincere boyfriend, Ed Koiki.

> *Two photos on the wall. Zoom in to close-up of a bride: Bonita. Fade in a song: 'I don't care if the sun don't shine, I don't care if the bells don't chime, just as long as you love me'.*

TREVOR: [*voice over*] On the tenth of October, nineteen fifty-nine, Ernestine Bonita Nehow married Edward Koiki Mabo at the

Methodist Church, Ingham, North Queensland.

A black-and-white photo, mid shot of the wedding couple. A black-and-white photo, wide shot of the wedding group. Dissolve to: a wide tracking shot down railway tracks. Sound effect: a train. Mid shot of the conductor. The song continues, '… North or south, east or west, you know I will stand the test, just as long as you love me'. The song fades out. Sound effect: the train's horn. A black-and-white photo, close-up of the young Bonita. Zoom out to medium-wide shot to reveal she is standing by railway tracks. Music.

BONITA: [*voice over*] So we went out to Jardine Valley. When I got up in the morning, I looked around. Oh, you could see for miles and miles. It was all bare and just mimosa bushes everywhere.

Wide shot of trucks and people in a field. Pan right. Medium-wide shot of men working in a field. Pan right with one man. Medium-wide shot of men working on a railway track a in field. A jackhammer and a mans legs.

TREVOR: [*voice over*] If the island of Mer was Eddie's first love, out in the dusty western plains of Queensland he found his second.

Mid shot of young Koiki. A black-and-white photo, close-up of Koiki. Zoom out to mid shot of a family group of four.

He would find in his family a refuge from the harsh realities of life in North Queensland.

Dissolve to: black-and-white photo, mid shot of Bonita and baby. Zoom in to close-up of Bonita and baby. Dissolve to: a black-and-white photo, mid shot of the baby. Zoom in to close-up. Dissolve to: a black-and-white photo, mid shot of two children.

BONITA: [*voice over*] This is Eddie and Maria out west … Marathon.

Close-up of an opened photo album. Close-up of Malita.

CHILD: [*out of view*] Uncle Eddie …

Medium close-up of the child flipping pages of the photo album.

Uncle Eddie, Uncle Eddie, Uncle Eddie.

EDDIE JNR: [*out of view*] In case you didn't get it the first time.

Fade music. Close-up of Eddie Jnr. Super: 'EDDIE MABO JNR'.

BONITA: [*out of view*] When we had Eddie, if ever he got sick or even when we come into town to do our shopping, we'd go to the hotels

and motels to see if we could get accommodation, just for the night
and we used to get knocked back. And always with the same, 'Got
no vacancies', even though they had rooms. They were just racist.

A black-and-white photo, medium close-up of infant Eddie Jnr and Maria.
Medium-wide shot of Eddie Jnr, Gail, Malita and a child. A black-and-
white photo, close-up of young Bonita and one of the kids. Zoom in to
extreme close-up. Close-up of Bonita in the present. Music. A black-and-
white photo, a child's feet. Tilt up to close-up.

So we'd come back the railway station and camped at the railway
station. It used to be really terrible and especially at winter time.

Close-up black-and-white photo, Koiki with a child. Zoom out to mid shot.
Wide tracking shot of hilly landscape. Music fades. Wide tracking shot of
houses. Wide tracking shot of joggers by the beach.

KOIKI: [*voice over*] When I settled in Townsville in nineteen sixty there
were only two Torres Strait families in town. Now we've got
something like eight thousand of them running around.

Archival black-and-white medium-wide shot of people on the footpath.
Archival black-and-white mid shot of people on the footpath. A black-and-
white photo, medium-wide shot of Koiki with Eddie Jnr. Zoom in to mid
shot.

HENRY REYNOLDS: [*voice over*] There was hostility to the fact that
people were moving into town. I think people still genuinely
thought that Aborigines in particular and to some extent
Islanders ...

Dissolve to: Close-up black-and-white photo, Bonita and child. Zoom in.
Close-up of Henry. Super: 'HENRY REYNOLDS, Friend'.

[*Sync*] ... Had smaller brains, were less intelligent. That is, the old
racism of the nineteenth century was still alive.

A black-and-white photo, close-up of young Koiki. Zoom out to mid shot.

KOIKI: [*voice over*] When I was only about twenty-one, I became
involved in street politics because of my belief that something had
to be done to try to alleviate the problems of the Aboriginal people,
and as a result of that I ended up in gaols and being arrested several
times.

Wide shot of Townsville port. Wide shot of people high up on a ship's deck.

Archival black-and-white wide shot of people and a crane. Archival black-and-white wide shot of people and berthed ships.

NOEL LOOS: [*voice over*] When he came into Townsville he worked at the Harbour Board and interacted with unionists there and, at that time, most leaders of the union movement were members of the Communist Party.

Mid shot of Noel.

[*Sync*] And this didn't worry Koiki, he didn't, as he said to me, he didn't even know what a communist was.

Mid shot of Henry Reynolds.

HENRY REYNOLDS: Well, the Communist Party was quite influential in Townsville, and it had been since the nineteen thirties.

Music. Close-up of Communist Party leaflets. Pan right across more.

[*Voice over*] And they had taken up the cause of Aborigines and Islanders very early. I mean, it was the Communist Party which first took, I would say, a modern view of the place of Aborigines and Islanders in Australia society in terms of correcting injustices and treating them not as an inferior race but as members of the proletariat.

Dissolve to: an archival black-and-white mid shot of a banner with pictures of Marx, Lenin and Ho Chi Minh. Dissolve to: a close-up of leaflets. Pan right over more leaflets. Dissolve to: an archival black-and-white wide shot of marchers. Dissolve to: a close-up of leaflets. Track forward above them. Dissolve to: a medium close-up of a note book. Zoom in. photo of marchers in close-up. Dissolve to: a black-and-white photo, medium-wide shot of men holding a banner: 'Wharfies Support Equal Rights for Aborigines'. Mid shot of Noel Loos.

NOEL LOOS: Also of course they had meetings and they invited speakers from the south and he was fascinated by their oratory and the fire of the their speeches.

An archival black-and-white mid shot of a union leader speaking publicly. Super impose the following three shots:

A black-and-white wide shot of a seated audience. A black-and-white wide shot from behind the audience. Pan right. A black-and-white Mid shot of a union leader standing, delivering a speech.

[*Voice over*] And one man who came up who was a very senior official of the Communist Party: Koiki said he wouldn't repeat the same word twice. And he went along to hear him speak ...

Dissolve to: a black-and-white photo, medium-wide shot of the audience applauding. Dissolve to: an archival black-and-white mid shot of a union leader speaking publicly. Fade music. Mid shot of Noel Loos.

[*Sync*] ... And people at the Harbour Board started referring to him as if he was a communist; a communist sympathiser.

A black-and-white photo of a banner. Pan right over the words: 'Vote Yes'. A song: 'Vote yes for Aborigines, they want to be Australians too. Vote yes and give them rights and freedoms just like me and you ...' A black-and-white photo, medium-wide shot of marchers and banners. Tilt up left to a banner: 'Vote Yes to give full rights to Aborigines and Torres Strait Islanders Referendum May 27 1967'.

TREVOR: [*voice over*] In nineteen sixty-seven, Eddie threw himself into the referendum campaign which would give Aboriginal and islander people the right to vote. Ninety percent of white Australia voted 'Yes'.

The song fades. An archival black-and-white medium-wide shot, people at a campaign table. Tilt up to two women. An archival black-and-white wide shot of a crowd. Leaflets on a table. A baby's face and the words: 'Right Wrongs Write Yes for Aborigines'. Archival black-and-white close-ups of several women. Pan left.

For the first time, indigenous people were recognised as citizens in their own land. For activists like Eddie, it was moment of optimism

A photo of Koiki in close-up. Zoom out to mid shot.

KOIKI: [*voice over*] And as a result of that it led to our group organising one of the biggest seminars held in Australia on black affairs, and we called it the Inter-racial Seminar.

The cover of a book: 'We the Australians: What is to follow the referendum?' Tilt down as the book is moved and opened. An archival black-and-white close-up of Koiki.

[*Sync*] ... About the only thing that will overcome that particular problem is if ...

MARGARET REYNOLDS: [*voice over*] Well, the aim was to insure that there was some action from the referendum in education, employment, in the legal area and housing.

Dissolve to: news print. Tilt up to the words: 'Aboriginal Race clash ahead seminar told'. Dissolve to: a black-and-white photo, medium-wide shot of women's faces. Pan right. Dissolve to: news print: 'White politics and an inter-racial seminar'. Zoom in. Dissolve to: news print. Tilt up to the headline: 'Native Speakers for Seminar'.

TREVOR: [*voice over*] But Eddie's political activism soon came to the attention of the authorities in Brisbane.

Dissolve to: a black-and-white photo, mid shot of Koiki at a lectern. Zoom out to medium-wide shot of a classroom. Close-up of Margaret Reynolds.

MARGARET REYNOLDS: The Queensland Government was very suspicious of it and we came under surveillance from Special Branch.

An extreme wide aerial view of the city at night. Zoom in to a wide shot of a well-lit road. Music.

[*Voice over*] We were followed, my home was broken into and even the Seminar itself was monitored to see who was coming and so his alleged paranoia about the Queensland Government did have a definite basis because he knew that he had been under close scrutiny.

Wide shot of buildings at night. Pan right, step printed. A black-and-white photo, medium-wide shot of seated women. Pan left. A black-and-white photo, close-up of Koiki. Zoom in to extreme close-up. Wide shot of a house at night. An archival black-and-white medium-wide shot of a crowd applauding. Pan left. Fade music.

ANNOUNCER: [*voice over*] Ladies and Gentlemen, it's time, the national leader of the Australian Labor Party, Mr Gough Whitlam.

Mid shot of a window at night.

GOUGH WHITLAM: [*voice over*] ... All of us as Australians are diminished ...

An archival black-and-white close-up of Gough Whitlam.

[*Sync*] ... While the Aborigines are denied their rightful place in this nation.

A photo, medium close-up of Koiki. Zoom in to close-up.

[*Voice over*] ... We ought to be angry with a deep determination ...

> *Official papers. Zoom in on the words: 'Mr. Koiki, President – Yumba Meta, Townsville'. Another document: 'Aboriginal Task Force'. Pages turning ...*

TREVOR: [*voice over*] With Gough Whitlam's election in nineteen seventy-two, Eddie's life became frenetic. Commonwealth money was flowing into Aboriginal and Islander organisations ... and Eddie was involved in all of them. The Legal Service, the Health Service, the Housing Co-op.

> *Close-up of Malita. Super: 'MALITA WEST, Daughter'.*

MALITA: When he started getting busy, that was it. You weren't allowed to laugh. You had to shut up; you weren't allowed to laugh loud because the neighbours would think we were idiots. 'What would they think, youse carrying on like this?' Not allowed to laugh loud.

> *Zoom out to mid shot.*

Me and Mel got sprung for doing, we were having spitting competition on the railing and we both got flogged. We weren't allowed to do that. I mean any parent wouldn't have let their kids' spit but ...

> *She laughs. Close-up of Gail Mabo.*

GAIL: Sometimes he'd come home a bit drunk and he and Mum would argue and I remember laying in bed just listening to them arguing

> *Photo, mid shot of Koiki. Zoom in to close-up.*

[*Voice over*] ... And he was that way where he was becoming a bit violent.

> *Close-up of Bonita. Photo, medium-wide shot of the family. Zoom in close-up of Koiki. Mid shot of Malita and Bonita. Zoom in on Bonita.*

BONITA: Well, he'd come home and, being the nearest thing to him, I suppose, he took it out on me. And there were many times, yeah, I ended up taking off and we'd come back again. But after a while he took it out on other things and left me alone, sort of thing. But I suppose that's life, eh?

A toothbrush. Zoom out to a mid shot of a child brushing paint onto the leaves of a tree. He leaves. Close-up of Gail.

GAIL: When he was overworked or he was under too much stress from the people who he was working with, he'd just come home and you'd hear him sitting there, just crying because he didn't know what to do.

Extreme close-up of eyes with glasses. A hand, writing. A photo, close-up of a young Koiki and Bonita. Zoom out, tilt down to a baby.

[*Voice over*] Sometimes Mum used to sit there as long as she could, sit and talk to him. Then if he couldn't think, he'd get up and dance. You could hear him singing. And if we were in the room doing whatever and we could hear him sing, we'd all join him with his songs. You'd hear the whole house start singing and he was like, from one room to the next room, it was just catchy. So in the end everyone was walking around the house singing the same song that Dad was singing.

Photos on a table. Zoom in to a photo of a girl in close-up. Close-up of Gail her child. Cut to mid shot.

GAIL: One of them just went, '*Au we tuli, au we tu-uli ...*'

Music and singing. Wide shot from the shore of water and the island. A bird flying. Dissolve to: a drawing of a seagull. Dissolve to: sky. Tilt down left to wide shot of the beach. Dissolve to: a panoramic drawing of the beach and hill. Pan left to people netting for fish.

[*Voice over*] You could always tell when he was homesick; he'd paint pictures of home. There were just things that reminded him of home, he just drew.

Dissolve to: a medium-wide shot of a woman on the beach, fishing. Dissolve to: a panoramic drawing of boats on the water. Pan left over the drawing. Dissolve to: a medium-wide shot of a boat on the water.

DONALD WHALEBOAT: [*voice over*] And he cried about it too. He was very emotional when you get to talk about Mer. He was homesick in the sense that he wanted to go back there.

Mid shot, pan right across people dancing. Pan left. Medium-wide shot of a boy fishing from the shore at dusk. The surface of the water.

ERIC WILLMOTT: [*voice* over] I mean, he was driven all his life by this

Island of his. It was a real obsession. This Isle of Mer was like where you go when you go to sleep.

Dissolve to: a drawing of two eyes. Tilt down to the rest of Koiki's face. Medium-wide shot at dusk of a person throwing a net. Waves on the shore. Mid shot of Gail and her child. Gail sings along as the music finishes.

GAIL: That was his favourite song.
CHILD: Look, there's a spider on your hand.
GAIL: That's all right; that's a money spider.

Close-up of the child looking at her hand.

[*Out of view*] See? And he just sing it all the and you knew where dad was when he'd sing that song.

Music and singing. Wide shot of palm trees, silhouetted at dusk. Mid shot of Koiki at a lectern. Fade out music and singing.

KOIKI: If I die, my kids will not be able to speak my language if I don't teach them at this stage. And of course that led to an idea that we must be able to retain our identity and culture, and this can only be taught to our kids through our own education system.

An archival black-and-white mid shot of a seated group singing.

TREVOR: [*voice over*] Eddie's determination that his children should share the songs and the language of Mer drove him to set up the first Black Community School in Australia in nineteen seventy-three.

An archival black-and-white mid shot, a woman and two kids. An archival black-and-white medium-wide shot, two adults and two kids in a classroom.

KOIKI: [*voice over*] … With Mrs Mabo are also doing craft work with other things. They seem very happy, particularly when they are engaged in craft work.

A black-and-white shot of a hand writing. Zoom out to mid shot of a child. A black-and-white shot of a book. Tilt up right to the child's face. A black-and-white wide shot of children dancing in a room. Zoom in on the kids.

TREVOR: [*voice over*] Before this, school had always been the place where black children learned white culture … and lost their own.

A drawing with labels in an Aboriginal language. Close-up of Donald

Whaleboat. Super: 'DONALD WHALEBOAT, Cousin'.

DONALD WHALEBOAT: He kept on saying to me, if we are able to have our own school where we could have the white curriculum is being taught there by the white teachers, we could have some white teachers come into the school but at the same time we can have the elders to come in and to teach our kids on the cultural side of things plus the language.

A black-and-white photo, a close-up two children. Zoom out to mid shot with their teacher. A black-and-white photo, a mid shot of three women. Pan left to more women and children in group. Music and singing. A black-and-white photo, a mid shot of two kids. Pan right to more kids.

And we could also teach them the crafts and how to plant gardens.

A black-and-white photo, a mid shot of three kids. Zoom out to medium-wide shot of five kids. A black-and-white photo, mid shot of Koiki seated with a woman.

TREVOR: [*voice over*] Eddie found the money and fought the battles. Netta contributed the TLC.

Mid shot of Eddie Jnr and Bonita. Pages of their school scrapbook turning. Fade out music and singing.

[*Voice over*] What were you doing there?

Medium close-up Eddie Jnr and Bonita.

BONITA: Oh, I was just a teacher's aide. And I was a mother to, aunt to all the children out there ...

A photo, a wide shot of a large group. Dissolve to: a photo, mid shot of a large group. Pan right across a row of people.

[*Voice over*] ... And in the afternoons some of the kids would want to come home, you know, to come and stay with us. I really got on good with the kids and they —

Medium close-up of Bonita and Eddie Jnr.

EDDIE JNR: You got on with everybody.
BONITA: ... And a lot of the children, too, came from broken homes and, you know ...

A photo, mid shot of a group of kids. Pan right across more children.

[*Voice over*] … Alcoholic parents and some of them were really wild when they started off there, but they were really tamed.

TREVOR: [*voice over*] What was it like to go there, Eddie? You went there, didn't you?

A black-and-white photo, close-up of Bonita. Tilt down right. Close-up of two kids.

EDDIE JNR: [*voice over*] What would happen is you, you'd be forced to participate. Whereas a kid who's not performing in a normal school would probably sit to the back of the class and just …

Close-up of Eddie Jnr.

[*Sync*] … 'Don't pick me, don't pick me', that kind of stuff …

A black-and-white photo, medium-wide shot of kids in a class room. Zoom in to mid shot of one girl.

[*Voice over*] … Whereas BCS, you were encouraged to speak your mind and participate.

Close-up of Eddie Jnr. Pan right to Bonita.

[*Sync*] Otherwise Auntie Netta would get you ….or Mum …

BONITA: I was there all the time so they couldn't muck up.

A black-and-white archival mid shot of Koiki.

KOIKI: We've been off our bums for the last three years trying to educate our kids …

A black-and-white photo, the words: 'Black Community School'. Zoom out to medium-wide shot of a bus covered with slogans.

[*Voice over*] … Yet no money is made available to be able to implement the things that we want to do.

MARGARET REYNOLDS: [*voice over*] The system, neither State nor Federal, ever accepted it. It was far too ahead of its time.

A black-and-white photo, medium-wide shot of the back of the bus, also covered in slogans. Close-up of Margaret Reynolds.

[*Sync*] But Eddie was enormously frustrated by the failure of the education bureaucracy to see that it was …

Mid shot black-and-white photo Koiki standing by the bus. Zoom in to close-up.

[*Voice over*] ... The answer to these questions of disadvantage and how children could and would learn if their own culture was part of the curriculum.

HENRY REYNOLDS: [*voice over*] There was a lot of hostility from the white community. It was seen as apartheid, it was seen as separatism, it was seen as threatening.

> *A black-and-white photo of a newspaper. Zoom in on the subheading: 'Black School Suspicious'. Another newspaper. Zoom in on: 'Surround Legality Community School'. A photo, medium-wide shot of women and kids marching with a banner: 'Give Us a Place In The Sun, the Traditional Landowners'. A photo, medium-wide shot of a group of kids. Newsprint. Zoom in on the words: 'Black School', etcetera ...*

NOEL LOOS: [*voice over*] And here was this little group of Islanders who set up an alternative education, but it was the black community school.

> *Close-up of Noel Loos.*

[*Sync*] The white authorities and the Townsville Daily Bulletin stressed the black, what they ignored was the fact that it was very much a community school, a community authority and that there were community schools all over Australia, you know, run by Greeks and other people.

> *A black-and-white archival mid shot of Koiki.*

KOIKI: There is a fear that, you know, when I started off, I'm teaching black power over there. Perhaps it would be better than teaching white power, wouldn't it?

> *Newsprint. Zoom in on the words: 'Racism', etcetera ... Close-up Henry Reynolds.*

HENRY REYNOLDS: There was also hostility amongst, certainly, the Aboriginal community of people who said, 'Look, on Palm Island' – where many of them had come from – 'we have always had to have special black schools. There was a black school and there was a white school. We have spent our lives trying to get a proper education for our kids and we want them to go to the proper school and not some second-rate black school'.

> *A photo, mid shot of Koiki sitting by a tree. Zoom in to close-up. Music.*

TREVOR: [*voice over*] In the midst of all his unpaid activism, Eddie still had to make a living. He found a job as a gardener at James Cook University.

Mid shot of Noel Loos.

NOEL LOOS: I regularly invited Koiki to come and speak to my race relations course which was called 'Race and Culture'.

Fade music. A black-and-white archival mid shot of Koiki lecturing.

KOIKI: There was completely nothing, nothing at all. We only had a tin of jam and a dugong spear to educate us.

Jump cut to mid shot. A black-and-white archival wide shot of Koiki talking in front of large class.

And is very shame for a country like this to be able to treat its indigenous people in this regard. How many black Australians can you see around the campus? It's nothing, it's a very shameful thing.

A black-and-white photo of two legs. Tilt up to Koiki's face.

NOEL LOOS: [*voice over*] So, he actually started participating in the academic life of James Cook.

Open books. Pan across more books.

HENRY REYNOLDS: [*voice over*] We would have lunch at least once or twice a week; he would tell me about growing up on the island and he would spend a lot of time in the library, reading all sorts of things. Although he had only had a very rudimentary education in English, he was a person who's main interest was in ideas. And when you talked about ideas and culture, he would glow.

A black-and-white photo, a wide shot of Koiki in the classroom demonstrating traditional Island implements. Zoom into Koiki.

TREVOR: [*voice over*] Eddie gave the academics and their students a first-hand taste of Islander culture. In return, they helped him understand the white man's system and the white man's law. And what he learned deeply offended his sense of justice.

A black-and-white photo, a mid shot of Koiki demonstrating traditional Island implements. Zoom out to a wide shot of the whole classroom. A black-and-white archival mid shot of Koiki. A black-and-white archival close-up of Koiki.

KOIKI: A hell of a lot of money has been spent on studies of black culture ...

HENRY REYNOLDS: [*voice over*] One of the things he always returned to about life on the island ...

> *Close-up of Henry.*

[*Sync*] ... Was the fact that he still had land there. And I asked him one day, 'But are you sure it will still be there when you go back? And he said, 'Oh yes, everybody knows it's Mabo land ...

> *A black-and-white photo, an extreme close-up of Koiki. Music.*

[*Voice over*] ... And my sister is looking after it. And as long as I want that land, it will be there for me when I go back.

> *Close-up of Henry Reynolds. Zoom in.*

[*Sync*] I said, 'Look, you do realise, do you, that it's not your land at all, because it's all Crown land'. And he looked at me with a mixture of horror and incredulity that anyone could doubt that it was his land.

> *A black-and-white photo, medium close-up of Koiki. Zoom in to close-up.*

[*Voice over*] It was as though I'd punched him in the face.

> *A pencil portrait of Koiki. Zoom in to the eyes.*

TREVOR: [*voice over*] For Eddie, it was a crucial turning point. He became obsessed with establishing his right to the Mabo land on Mer.

> *A mouth harp being played. Zoom out to close-up of Koiki. Close-up of Bonita.*

BONITA: I think it really affected him. He said, 'No Bs are going to stop me from, you know, my land.' He said, 'Over my dead body!'

> *Pan right with the words as they spew out of a telex machine..*

TREVOR: [*voice over*] In nineteen seventy-three, Eddie tried to go back to his island for the first time in fifteen years. His father Benny was ill ... and only one of Eddie's seven children had ever met their grandfather.

> *A black-and-white photo, close-up of Benny Mabo and his grandson. Tilt up right to Koiki's face.*

But the Murray Island Council, which had exiled him fifteen years earlier, was still under the sway of the Queensland Department of Aboriginal Affairs.

Mid shot of the same black-and-white photo of Benny Mabo, Koiki Mabo and Eddie Mabo Jnr as a child. Words spew out of a telex machine: '... permission not granted for your wife and family to visit ...'

And under state law, Eddie needed the Council's permission to return home.

Close-up of Bonita.

BONITA: ... Because Koiki was involved in all this political stuff down south, so they didn't want him to go back to the island and spread anything like that up there.

Words punching from the telex. Pan to follow the type.

[*Voice over*] And they sent back telegrams to us saying, 'Permission not granted' to see the old fella.

Close-up of Henry Reynolds.

HENRY REYNOLDS: I suspect the Queensland Government told leading men on the island that Eddie Mabo was a dangerous person and was a communist. And of course that was enough in those days to damn you in the eyes of many many people, both black and white.

A black-and-white photo, close-up of Eddie. Zoom in to his eyes.

[*Voice over*] And I'm sure the Queensland Government knew of his activities because the Special Branch was really quite active in Townsville at that time.

BONITA: [*voice over*] And then we got another telegram after that to say that the old fella died.

Music out. Close-up of Bonita.

[*Sync*] And when the telegram came here and Eddie was at work so when he came home and I gave him the telegram, oh. Man, it was like showing a bull a red rag. He was that upset, you know ...

Close-up of Eddie Jnr.

EDDIE JNR: That added fuel to the fire for dad; he became more determined to get us to Mer and to secure what he knew was his.

Tracking shot, forward over the water. Music. Waves on a beach.

KOIKI: [*voice over*] I believe the islands were mine, nobody could stop me from going there. In nineteen seventy-seven I hired a boat and went across there with my family.

Wide shots of a man on a vehicle, trees, people on a path.

I was expected to be arrested by the Queensland police, but when my people saw me no one complained.

Medium close-up of James Rice and his wife on a motor bike. Mid shot, from behind. Close-up of the pair from the front.

JAMES RICE: [*voice over*] Koiki used to come and have a cup of tea and talked about how we got to get it right, how we were going to set our people free from the Government, to live on their own land, so nobody will stop them. He'd cry for it.

Wide shot of the vehicle on a dirt road. Pan left. Zoom out to a wide shot of the graveyard.

TREVOR: [*voice over*] That visit in nineteen seventy-seven marked the start of the great battle of Eddie Mabo's life. It started beside his father's grave ... and didn't end until he was buried in his own.

Tilt down a headstone: 'In Loving Memory of our dear Father, Uncle ...' The grave. Fade to black.

Intertitle: 'The Battle of His Life'.

Fade up wide shot of the High Court building.

TREVOR: [*voice over*] In nineteen eighty-two, Eddie and four other Islanders filed a writ in the High Court of Australia. By claiming customary ownership of their ancestral lands on Murray Island, they were taking on the most fundamental tenet of Australian land law.

Tracking shot of the ceiling of the High Court. Wide shot of stairs and escalators. Portraits of judges on the wall. A portrait, close-up of a judge. Fade out music. Close-up of Bryan Keon-Cohen. Super: 'BRYAN KEON-COHEN, Barrister Mabo Case'.

BRYAN KEON-COHEN: The law when we started this case in nineteen eighty-two that no Aboriginal/Islander communities enjoyed traditional rights to land. This was the doctrine of *terra nullius*, which had been accepted by Australian courts as existing since seventeen eighty-eight throughout the whole of Australia.

Mid shot.

That nobody enjoyed rights in the land except the Crown. And therefore it was open slather to expand settlement, to enact laws ...

A black-and-white archival wide shot of police.

[*Voice over*] ... Without having to pay any regard to anyone else's pre-existing rights in those lands.

A black-and-white archival wide shot of the police dragging and Aboriginal person. Chanting: 'Land rights! Land rights!' An archival black-and-white mid two-shot, police grabbing people.

TREVOR: [*voice over*] To Eddie Mabo, the land rights movement of the seventies and eighties was on the wrong track.

Medium-wide three-shot of marchers.. Chanting: 'Land rights now! Land rights now!'

It was not for white governments, he felt, to grant or withhold rights to traditional Aboriginal land. He was determined to establish, in the courts, that the land had been stolen in the first place.

Wide shot tracking backwards before three people. One walks into mid shot. Close-up of Henry Reynolds.

HENRY REYNOLDS: Well, Eddie believed profoundly in the justice of his cause, that it was his land and that there was no doubt about that. But most indigenous Australians, Aborigines and Islanders also believed that the land was theirs. What Eddie also believed was that the Australian courts could be used and would deliver justice ...

Mid shot of the statue of justice. Tilt down left to a mid shot of Koiki and another plaintiff. Zoom out to a wide shot of the group getting a professional photo taken.

[*Voice over*] ... Which a great many Aborigines and Islanders didn't think. So those two things in tandem were what made Eddie so distinctive and important.

Flash. Sound effect: a camera flashbulb. A black-and-white photo, wide shot of the group of plaintiffs and their barrister. Wide shot of the photographer taking a photo of the four men under the statue.

TREVOR: [*voice over*] Eddie was under no illusions about the scale of the task.

Flash. Sound effect: a camera flashbulb. A black-and-white photo, mid shot of the four men under the statue. Close-up of two faces. Pan right across more people to a mid shot of two men.

He and his co-plaintiffs were facing the combined resources of the Queensland and Commonwealth Governments. He told me he saw himself as David challenging Goliath.

Close-up of Eddie and Bonita. Fade to black.

Music and singing. Fade up an underwater shot of a school of fish. Wide shot of a man throwing a fishing net. Underwater the net comes down on the sardines. Close-up of a man. Zoom out and pan left. Mid shot of a man walking.

In nineteen eighty-nine, after seven long years of legal argument and government obstruction, the lawyers appeared on Murray Island. They'd come to challenge – or to uphold – the myth that had justified the takeover of a continent.

Wide shot of two barristers approaching. Mid shot of a man and woman. Wide shot from behind of two men walking. Wide shot from in front of a man walking a dirt road. Mid shot of a priest and people in Church. Mid shot under water of the netted fish being dragged up. Mid shot of a man pulling the net from the water. Pan left with a man walking.

Despite fifty thousand years of occupation, the law of *terra nullius* maintained, the indigenous people of Australia had no concept of law, or ownership, before the arrival of white men in black gowns.

Medium-wide shot of people in a court room. Medium-wide shot of barristers standing and sitting. Medium-wide shot of people in a court room. Zoom out to wide shot: more people sitting. Wide shot from behind of people standing around the court room. Fade out music and singing.

Now, the High Court of Australia had ordered Mr Justice Moynihan, of the Supreme Court of Queensland, to gather evidence on its behalf, and report back on the facts of the Mabo case.

Wide shot of lawyers entering the court room from the right. Medium-wide shot of a man standing, talking. Mid shot of Justice Moynihan at a desk.

Super: 'JUSTICE MARTIN MOYNIHAN, Supreme Court of Queensland'.

JUSTICE MOYNIHAN: It is perhaps apposite that I remark that this is an historic occasion. It is the first sitting of the Supreme Court of Queensland on Murray Island. The case is an important one involving, as it does, people of Murray Island pursuing claims against the state of Queensland and the Commonwealth of Australia.

Medium close-up, a row of Islander men. Medium close-up of a man, listening. Mid shot of Justice Moynihan. Medium close-up of two men.

Sitting here ...

Medium close-up of Koiki, Bonita and a man. Medium close-up of the man speaking. Mid shot of a woman with a tape recorder. Close-up of the man.

KOIKI: [*voice over*] As far as the Murray Islanders are concerned, it's very exciting, and we feel that we've made history ...

Mid shot of Koiki and Eddie Jnr. Zoom in right to close-up of Koiki.

[*Sync*] ... In terms of the highest court in Queensland coming out to an Aboriginal or an Islander community to sit in our public hall and listen to us.

Medium-wide shot of the Court Bailiff walking out the door.

COURT BAILIFF: Sam Passi ...

Wide shot of Sam Passi walking to the right. Pan to wide shot of Sam Passi walking to the court.

[*Out of view*] Sam Passi ...

Mid shot of Koiki and two witnesses. Medium close-up of two people. Close-up of Koiki.

KOIKI: [*subtitled*] You'll be next in court. Somebody will cross-examine you. Just wait outside; someone will call you in.

FATHER DAVE PASSI: [*voice over*] Koiki had been away from the land for so long, but he was still a true Murray Islander.

Medium-wide shot of a man holding a baby and another man. Close-up of Koiki. Medium-wide shot of Father Dave Passi with the island behind him. Super: 'FATHER DAVE PASSI, Co-Plaintiff'.

[*Sync*] I see Koiki's role as being very important. We needed a leader who could lead us in this fight.

Medium-wide shot of the plaintiffs and their barrister.

[*Voice over*] He had white man's education but he was also very much educated in his island culture.

Medium-wide shot of the plaintiffs, Koiki on the right.

TREVOR: [*voice over*] I was filming with Eddie while the hearings took place.

Mid shot of Trevor, sitting. Mid shot of Bonita and a child. Medium-wide shot of a group of men.

It was here on Mer that our friendship But he hadn't lost his lifelong ability to make enemies as well as friends.

Mid shot of a group of witnesses.

BRYAN KEON-COHEN: [*voice over*] Eddie Mabo was an agitator, he was a free thinker, he was prepared to commit himself to a cause which he believed to be just and beneficial to his community.

Mid shot of Bryan.

[*Sync*] Like many political leaders, he was a strong egocentric personality; he believed in himself and in his own abilities and intellect.

Mid shot of Eddie and Bryan pointing. Pan right with the men. Wide shot from behind of a group walking.

[*Voice over*] He, Eddie Mabo, believed that what he was doing was correct and the rest of them could like it or lump it.

Wide shot of a group approaching alone a bush path.

TREVOR: [*voice over*] Eddie conducted the lawyers around the island, meticulously pointing out the boundaries of the plots he claimed as his: no fewer than thirty-six of them in all.

Medium-wide shot of the court moving left to right through the bush. Pan with them. Mid shot of the court standing in the bush. Pan left to more people moving away. Music and singing. Wide shot of tractors approaching down a path. Mid shot of the court on a cart pulled by a tractor right to left. Wide shot of bush and ocean. Track right. Dissolve to: close-up of a hand-

drawn map and words. Tilt down right. Dissolve to: a medium-wide shot tractor approaching. Mid shot of two men. Pan right to Koiki. Pan left as he goes into the bush and points to an obscured 'boundary marker'. Fade out music and singing.

KOIKI: [*voice over*] I want to show the judge the boundary markers that has been in place as far as I can remember. And as far as according to my dad's comments, as far as he could remember and it's important that he actually see the things himself.

Medium-wide shot of Justice Moynihan in a hat looking at papers. Mid shot as he walks away. Tracking shot which tilts down to a pile stones: a boundary marker. Tilt up to Koiki digging and pointing.

[*Sync*] This is the one here. And from here, it goes straight into the bush about one hundred yards. And this is the boundary line here.

Dissolve to: writing on a map. Tilt down left on the page. Dissolve to: a mid shot of Koiki talking and pointing. Mid shot of the group in the bush. Mid shot of Koiki talking and pointing.

These sorts of things that can be seen all over this island. Other families have constructed these things, not just lately but over many years to mark their boundaries off from another family. And it's just heaps of rocks, it's small rocks off their garden and they're picked up and they put them in heaps on the boundary line, like this. And that can be seen all over Murray Island.

Wide shot of the court on the beach. Medium-wide shot from behind the judge at water's edge. Wide shot of a bird flying over the beach. Medium-wide shot of people on the beach, pointing.

TREVOR: [*voice over*] But there were plenty of Islanders who questioned the validity of Eddie's claims.

Wide shot of the group on the beach.

The traditional laws of inheritance were complex, and until the arrival of missionaries there were no written records.

A black-and-white archival photo, a wide shot of a large hut on the beach. Zoom in to a person by the hut. Music and singing. Dissolve to: a black-and-white photo, close-up of a man. Pan right to another man. Dissolve to: a black-and-white photo, wide shot of a group in traditional dress. Dissolve to: a black-and-white photo, wide shot of a group of people. Pan left over the group.

KOIKI: [*voice over*] The land usually gets passed on from father to son, by word of mouth, that is our only way of passing from one generation to another.

> *Mid shot of two men. Zoom in left to medium close-up Koiki. Fade out music and singing.*

[*Sync*] Before the father dies, he takes his children through and teaches them where the exact boundary lines are. That of course is done with the agreement of the neighbouring clan.

> *Wide shot of Mr Depoma with his walking stick on the beach. Zoom out. Pan right with him.*

TREVOR: [*voice over*] So you think Eddie Mabo is claiming too much land?

MR DEPOMA: [*voice over, subtitled*] He can go and claim another family's land. Not here, this place. Not my uncle's place.

> *Mid shot of Mr Depoma. Super: 'MR. DEPOMA, Witness for Queensland Government.*

[*Sync*] He's got no claim for this land, or in the bush. He's only got one garden plot, at Aum. That's from his grandmother.

Music. Writing: 'E. K. Koiki, 23 Hibiscus St, Cranbrook NQ'. Pan left to the words: 'Dear Mr. Dipoma …'

KOIKI: [*voice over*] Dear Mr Dipoma,

> *Dissolve to: the hand written letter. Tilt down the words. Fade music. Dissolve to: more handwriting. Pan right over the words.*

… your letters are full of what normally drops off in your toilet after a good feed.

> *Dissolve to: handwriting. Pan right over the words.*

TREVOR: [*voice over*] For years he'd been conducting vigorous disputes by mail from Townsville about who owned what on Murray Island.

> *More handwriting. Pan right. Handwriting. Tilt down.*

KOIKI: [*voice over*] My adoptive parents claim me alone as their son. You have no claim for that land. Now I'm telling you to move out or you'll be thrown out by force.

Close-up of several barristers. Zoom out to medium-wide shot of a group of people in the makeshift courtroom.

TREVOR: [*voice over*] The Queensland barristers were quick to seize on these land disputes.

Mid shot of a man sitting, typing by a tree. Medium-wide shot of a group of women sitting outside.

Five of their nine witnesses were called specifically to challenge Eddie's claims to particular blocks of land.

Medium-wide shot of three people outside the courtroom. Close-up two people. Mid shot of a woman barrister crouching, talking to Mr Depoma outside the courtroom.

WOMAN: These people in here are taking too long, too long.

Medium close-up of a woman with a fan. Medium close-up of two men. Medium-wide shot of five people sitting in chairs outside. Medium close-up of two women talking.

PAUL SMITH: [*voice over*] I was the lawyer for Queensland involved in the case. Eddie was claiming a very large area of land on Murray Island ...

Close-up of Paul Smith. Super: 'PAUL SMITH, Crown Law Department Queensland'.

[*Sync*] ... And it caused particular trouble to a number of Murray Islanders who through their own personal histories and their own traditions claimed that it was their own parents and grandparents who passed that very same blocks of land on to them and not to Eddie Mabo.

Wide shot of people walking by outside the court. Pan right. Close-up of many faces passing.

KOIKI: [*voice over*] There are Murray Islanders appearing for the Queensland Government, but of course they are not saying ...

Mid shot of Koiki sitting outside.

[*Sync*] ... That the land belongs to Queensland; they are saying that they are the owners of their plots of land which of course demonstrates to me, or anyone listening to them, that there is a system in existence.

Medium-wide shot of dancers. Music and singing.

TREVOR: [*voice over*] And that, of course, was the essential point of the Mabo case. Murray Island had never been *terra nullius*.

Mid shot of two seated men. Medium-wide shot of the dancers. Zoom in the dancers' headdresses.

Eddie and the other plaintiffs spoke passionately in court about Malo, the God who had come to the island in the form of an octopus, to unite the eight tribes of Mer. Malo gave them laws and ceremonies to govern their lives.

Medium close-up of a man with his hands behind his head, watching the dancers. Medium close-up of two seated men. Medium close-up of two men clapping. A shark headdress. Zoom out to Medium-wide shot. Fade out music and singing. Wide shot of a man approaching in shade. Pan left with him. Super: 'KABA NOAH'.

Many elders could still recite the commandments of Malo.

Mid shot of Kaba Noah sitting outside, holding the sacred drum of Malo.

KABA NOAH: [*subtitled*] 'Tag' means 'hand', 'teter' means 'leg': you can't just wander across the village. This is our traditional culture. The law of Malo.

Music. Close-up of the drum. Close-up of Kaba Noah. Music.

[*Subtitled*] You must get permission from the owner before you catch a fish in a fish trap. It means you can't just wander in the village. This is the law of Malo.

Music. Wide shot of a Malo ceremony at the edge of the forest. Close-up of a masked face. Pan left with him. Mid shot of a group of men sitting on the ground. Mid shot of the dancers.

KOIKI: [*voice over*] My dad was actually an authority on Malo's law itself because it was actually based here at the very place we are sitting. My grandfather taught me ...

Mid shot of Koiki. Fade out music and singing.

[*Sync*] ... Not to walk on anybody else's properties. Now the same thing was reinforced by my dad, who would say that you must withhold your feet from entering someone else's property because it's against Malo's law, but of course we have a lot of problems that we have to convince the white law to take those into account.

Wide shot of people standing in the court room. Medium close-up of Justice Moynihan.

JUSTICE MOYNIHAN: … For making available the facilities of the island to us in order that we might sit here.

Medium-wide shot of women and flowers. Music and singing. Wide shot of a group outside. Mid shot of a little boy. Mid shot of people, a photographer amongst them. Medium-wide shot of people getting food at the table outside. Medium-wide shot of people with coconut drinks. Mid shot of two women and a man talking. Medium-wide shot of five people in flower hats. Close-up of Koiki.

TREVOR: [*voice over*] Undoubtedly, Eddie enjoyed his time in the limelight on Murray Island.

Mid shot of Koiki and his lawyers in hats with coconut drinks.

But it was a short episode in a long ordeal.

Fade out music and singing. Wide shot of a large road in Brisbane. Traffic sound effect. Close-up of a road sign: 'Turbot St'. Medium-wide shot of the passing crowd on the footpath. Pan left with Koiki's group.

TREVOR: [*voice over*] Many of Justice Moynihan's hearings were held in Brisbane, where Eddie faced days of gruelling cross-examination by the Queensland Government's well-briefed lawyers.

Dissolve to: handwriting. Pan right over the words: 'witness box'. Dissolve to: medium-wide shot of Koiki, Bonita and Eddie Jnr walking. Pan right with them. Wide shot of a group of people approaching on the footpath. Wide shot of a group of people walking right to left along a footpath. Pan left with them. Zoom out to a wide shot of an imposing building with the sign: 'The Law Courts'.

BRYAN KEON-COHEN: [*voice over*] Queensland had done a very large body of research on him and on other witnesses. And that over ten days in the witness box, there's not many aspects of your life that remain hidden from view. And one of the lines of attack, for example …

Mid shot of Bryan Keon-Cohen.

[*Sync*] … Was on the central proposition that he had inherited land from his parents by reason that he had been adopted, customary style, to his adopted father, and thus, by reason of that adoption, the father's rights and interest in land passed down to him, the adopted child.

Medium-wide shot of three bewigged legal counsel at a table. Close-up of another lawyer. Wide shot of the court room: seven people seated.

PAUL SMITH: [*voice over*] Well, it was important from a legal aspect to show that ...

Close-up of Paul Smith.

[*Sync*] ... The land which was claimed specifically by Eddie Mabo, who needed to be a Mabo to be able to claim that land. So Queensland set out to establish who Eddie Mabo actually was; was he actually a Mabo or did he belong to another family group?

Wide shot of the courtroom. There is a long table with barristers and people behind.

COURT BAILIFF: Silence and all stand, please.

All rise. Music. Medium-wide shot of the room. The judge enters. A medium-wide shot pans across the standing crowd.

BRYAN KEON-COHEN: [*voice over*] They presented social security cards to him for the proposition ...

Mid shot of Bryan Keon-Cohen.

[*Sync*] 'Listen, Mr Mabo, you were not adopted under island custom, you weren't adopted at all.'

A black-and-white photo, a mid shot of Koiki's adoptive father and mother. Zoom out to a family shot of four adults and a baby. A photo, close-up of a bewigged Bryan Keon-Cohen. Tilt down left to close-up of Koiki.

[*Voice over*] 'You merely went to live with that family to enable those adoptive parents to claim extra social security.' They were suggesting that, 'Listen, your honour, you can't believe this guy, and everything he says: it's just not credible and his evidence should be discounted'.

Wide tracking shot of cars along a bridge. Mid shot of Koiki and Bonita. Fade music.

TREVOR: [*voice over*] For Eddie, the case was not just a personal challenge, but a financial one too.

> *Wide shot tracking left, looking up at a building. Pan right with a taxi.*

Constantly travelling between Torres Strait, Townsville and Brisbane, he spent most of the nineteen eighties unemployed.

> *Dissolve to: a pan, right, across open books. Dissolve to: hands flipping papers. Dissolve to: a written page is lifted to reveal the words: 'Education Qualifications'. Close-up of documents. Dissolve to: a typed document.*

BONITA: [*voice over*] You know, he couldn't hold down a job because he was away too much, so he ended up going on the dole. We never starved.

> *Close-up of Bonita.*

[*Sync*] Sometimes we had to rake enough for his bus fare to go anywhere, and we sort of either left the house payment to give him the money to go. Then we would be behind in that. So many a time we got letters from the bank, but anyway we managed to catch up with it somehow or other.

> *Mid shot of Bonita and Eddie in a taxi.*

[*Voice over*] But we hung in there with him.

TREVOR: [*voice over*] In September nineteen eighty-nine, seven years after the first writ was filed, the court in Brisbane adjourned. Justice Moynihan retired to consider and write his findings for the High Court of Australia and Eddie retired to the family in Townsville, and the children who'd grown up while he fought his case. He found he had his own weighty judgments to deliver.

> *Medium-wide shot traffic approaching. Pan left with the action. Wide shot of a city road. Medium-wide shot of two people at a barbecue. Medium-wide shot of two people and a baby at the barbecue. Zoom in to close-up of the baby. Mid shot of two seated women eating. Close-up of Danny West. Super: 'DANNY WEST, Son in Law'.*

DANNY WEST: When I actually went up to ask him for his daughter's hand in marriage, that's where I actually got the shock of my life was that he said 'You know, if she was up in the island, that her husband was already picked out'.

> *Close-up of Malita.*

[*Out of* view] I said, 'Oh, right, okay'.

Close-up of Danny. Pan left to a close-up of Malita. Pan right to close-up of Danny.

He said, 'Yeah, but since she's here in Townsville there's nothing really I can do about it' … so that was basically it. I took that as a 'Yes'. I suppose that was it, wasn't it? That was his 'Yes'.

MALITA: No, then it was 'It's not a shotgun wedding?'

TREVOR: [*out of view*] So he would have preferred that you married a Murray Islander?

MALITA: He would have preferred if I married a real black boy, 'black' as in black skin, none of these half-caste ones, a real black one.

DANNY: Yeah, when we started getting into it, he was telling me how strong the islander genes were compared to the Aboriginal genes. I was shocked; I didn't know what to do, I was dumbfounded. I didn't have any come-back for it. Other than I suppose if you look at our kids they have sort of taken after me, haven't they? So it's the strength in those islander genes. I'll cause racial division here

MALITA: [*out of view*] Yes.

TREVOR: [*out of view*] But then, you obviously got close.

MALITA: He soon passed that.

DANNY: Once that was gone, yeah, it was excellent, excellent, we got on well. I spent a bit of time with him on his boat …

A photo, medium-wide shot of Eddie by his boat. Zoom in to mid shot of Koiki.

[*Voice over*] … That was sort of where he lived when he was here, working on his boat, bit by bit.

Music. A photo, close-up of Koiki. A photo, mid shot of Trevor and his family.

TREVOR: [*voice over*] Eddie's obsession with his boat helped him cope with the waiting. He'd ring me every so often, to tell me he'd pulled out the engine, or was putting in a new deck. 'What about the court case?' I'd ask. 'Still nothing', he'd say …

A photo, close-up of Koiki smiling. Zoom in and fade to black.

… 'But I'm not worried. Moynihan's has got plenty to think about.'

Fade up on a copy of Justice Moynihan's findings. Zoom out as a hand turns the pages.

But Justice Moynihan was about to fire a salvo which threatened to sink the Mabo case. In November nineteen ninety, he presented his findings to the High Court of Australia.

Dissolve to: a few words of type on paper: 'Eddie Mabo's Claim ...' Dissolve to: the open book. Dissolve to: type on the page.

BRYAN KEON-COHEN: The result was that his claims to land on Murray Island were denied because Justice Moynihan determined ...

Pan right over the words: '... adoption of Eddie ...'

... That he was not adopted in accordance with island custom and tradition and therefore had not inherited those lands from his adoptive father.

Dissolve to: arms turning the pages of the book. Fade music. Close-up Bryan Keon Cohen.

BRYAN KEON-COHEN: This was devastating for Eddie Mabo. It attacked his sense of self. It amounted to the Australian legal system saying to Eddie Mabo ...

A black-and-white photo, mid shot of two seated men. Zoom in to close-up of Koiki.

[*Voice over*] ... You're not what you claim to be and you don't enjoy the traditional rights and interests on Murray Island.

Medium-wide shot photo, three men at a table. Zoom in to close-up of Koiki. Close-up of Bonita.

BONITA: He just swore and carried on, as he usually did when he got upset. 'I'm a Mabo and that's it! Nobody is going to change that.'

Wide shot of the High Court building. Sound effect of traffic. Wide shot of the building on the lake.

TREVOR: [*voice over*] In May nineteen ninety-one the High Court held the final hearing on the Mabo case in Canberra.

Mid shot of Bryan Keon-Cohen in front of the High Court building.

BRYAN KEON-COHEN: The lawyers arrived here from Melbourne and Perth, Eddie arrived by bus from Brisbane. He was quietly confident. He, I think, with all of us was relieved that the final chapter was about to start.

A photo, Close-up of Koiki's barristers. Pan right to Koiki and another barrister.

[*Voice over*] There was no question other than we all believed we had a just cause and that we would get a reasonable hearing from the High Court.

Wide shot from above the benches in the court room.

TREVOR: [*voice over*] These seven judges would consider Justice Moynihan's findings and then determine whether Murray islanders had a customary right to the land they lived on, which Australia's common law should recognise.

Medium-wide shot of a woman handing papers to the judges. Mid shot from behind of a lawyer flipping pages of a notebook. Close-up of a woman at the bench. A portrait of a judge. Zoom in to the face. Wide shot of the interior of the building. Wide shot out through a very large window.

HENRY REYNOLDS: [*voice over*] I last saw Eddie on the day of the last hearing of the case.

Close-up of the kangaroo-and-emu coat of arms on the window. Wide shot overview of books and people in the court room. Zoom out wider.

We sat in the court together throughout the hearings. He felt that this meeting of the full High Court in Canberra ...

Close-up of Henry Reynolds.

[*Sync*] ... Was the final recognition of the importance and the justice of his crusade.

Music. Close-up photo of Koiki with a white beard. Zoom in to extreme close-up.

[*Voice over*] He was on a high and he was glowing. But glowing with a sense of achievement, I think, that, after all this time, he'd come from nowhere.

Fade to black.

TREVOR: [*voice over*] None of us knew how long the High Court would take to decide on Eddie's case ... and none of us knew he was dying.

Fade up to close-up of Gail. Fade music.

GAIL: I rang him up and said, 'Hi Dad, how you doing?' And he said, 'Oh, I'm all right'. And I said, [*in a croaky voice*] 'Hey, you're talking like this? What are you talking like that for?' He said, 'Ah, I got laryngitis'. And I said, [*in a croaky voice*] 'Okay, then, put me back to Mum'. He said, 'Stop making fun'. I said, 'Oh, but you sound really funny'.

Medium close-up of Bonita.

BONITA: He'd walk around the yard and he'd hit his hip or kick his leg too. I don't know what sort of relief it gave him but he used to do that a lot.

Handwriting. Tilt down the page. Music. Dissolve to: a tighter shot. Pan right over the words: 'To Doctor ...'

[*Voice over*] So we went down to the specialist and then he made arrangements for the hospital to be admitted straight away.

An X-ray. Tilt down. Close-up of Bonita.

[*Sync*] Next day, they said he had cancer.

Extreme close-up of print: '... Thursday 2 ...' Pan right to script: '... Tvill Hospital ...' Dissolve to: a handwritten page. Tilt down.

KOIKI: [*voice over*] I laid in bed thinking about the future. How I would like it to be, even if I am not there.

Wide shot of a person standing in a boat on still water. Track right. Script: '... I thought ...' Pan right over the words.

I thought about the struggles I'd been through all the past years since nineteen sixty three to the beginning of nineteen ninety-two.

A school of fish, underwater. Dissolve to: a black-and-white photo, close-up of Bonita as a bride. Zoom in.

I also thought about how my wife was the most important person in my life. The most adorable person, a friend also, a most wonderful lover.

Dissolve to: a black-and-white photo, mid shot of Koiki and Bonita. Zoom in. Dissolve to: a photo, close-up of Koiki and Bonita.

And we loved every minute of our lives together. I was classed as her lackey and she could push me around at home any which way.

Dissolve to: a photo, mid shot of Koiki and Bonita in summer clothes.
Dissolve to: a photo, mid shot of Koiki and Bonita. Dissolve to: script on
paper. Pan right across the words: '... loved it.'

I just loved it, every bit of it.

Follow a seagull in the air. Close-up of Bonita.

BONITA: Then the doctor said that they were going to send him down
to Brisbane.

Step-printed wide shot: a hospital corridor. Fade to white.

[*Voice over*] We went straight to the Radium Centre and they started
doing radium on him.

Fade up on a blue, white and black abstract.

GAIL: [*voice over*] So I talked to him again and he was ...

Close-up of Gail.

[*Whispering*] ... Like you couldn't really hear him; he was whispering.

Fade to white. Fade up on an intravenous drip. Tilt down.

BONITA: [*voice over*] That morning he, every two hours, right at nine
o'clock, he'd ask me the time.

Close-up of Bonita.

[*Sync*] It wasn't long after, he just started gasping for breath, you
know. And I didn't even give it a thought about putting a mask on
him at all. So I just sort of put my arms around him and grabbed
him because he was gasping for breath and ...

A school of fish, underwater.

[*Voice over*] ... Kicking himself up towards the head of the bed.

Close-up of Bonita.

[*Sync*] And it's only just recently it sort of hit me that he really did
die in my arms, you know.

Fade up from white to a photo, close-up of Koiki in a suit jacket. Zoom out
to a mid shot with two other men. Fade to white. Fade up to a black-and-
white photo, extreme close-up of the younger Koiki. Zoom out to close-up.
Fade to white. Fade up to a black-and-white photo, close-up of Koiki as a

very young man. Zoom out to mid shot. Fade to white. Fade up on a step-printed white cross in earth, flowers being put on the grave. Close-up of the yellow flowers. Tilt up the cross to the words: 'Edward Koiki Mabo'. Medium-wide shot of the family approaching the grave.

[*Voice over*] His wishes were to take him back to the island.

Medium close-up of Bonita with a picture of Koiki behind her.

[*Sync*] I just found it too hard to do that. I didn't want to part with him.

A black-and-white photo, mid shot of Bonita and daughters by the white cross.

TREVOR: [*voice over*] Eddie Koiki Mabo was laid to rest in Townsville Cemetery.

Wide shot of a truck driving through the cemetery. Zoom out to extreme wide shot of the surrounding bush and hills.

But he would not be allowed to rest in peace.

Pink flowers in a vase. Zoom in to a photo of Koiki on the wall behind.

Only five months after Koiki's death the High Court delivered its judgement on the Mabo case.

FIRST FEMALE REPORTER: [*voice over*] Today in Canberra, the High Court ruled that residents of the Murray Islands in the Torres Strait owned customary title ...

FIRST MALE REPORTER: [*voice over*] Australia has recognised the legal existence of Aborigines ...

SECOND MALE REPORTER: [*voice over*] This is the most important court decision in the two-hundred-years history of white occupation in this country ...

A photo of a home-made banner: 'Mabo "v" QLD, We Won'. Tilt up to Bonita's smiling face. Words on a television screen: 'Landmark Case'. Pan right to a presenter.

THIRD MALE REPORTER: ... A moral victory as well as having great significance for land rights.

Medium close-up of a young man, arms raised in victory. Zoom out slightly. Close-up of Gail.

GAIL: I remember sitting in the car and the first time I heard it, I just cried. People walking past were just looking at me and I was just bawling. And I thought, 'Well, I don't care ... I'm happy and I'm sad all wrapped into one and no one's going to stop me'. I said, 'I'm happy, but I wish my dad was here to reap the benefits of his deed'.

Music. Gold print on the red cover of the High Court judgement. Fade to black.

TREVOR: [*voice over*] The High Court decided that it didn't need to rule on the validity of Eddie Mabo's claims to particular bits of land on Murray Island. The real issues, it declared, were these:

Fade up on an arm turning the pages of the book. Zoom in. Dissolve to: type on paper. Tilt down the page. Dissolve to: a tighter shot. Pan right, across the words: 'Recognised by the Crown'.

Did the community of Murray Island have a system of land ownership which pre-dated white conquest? And if so, was that system still valid? The Court answered 'Yes' to both questions.

Dissolve to: medium-wide shot of four people in a yellow motorboat. Dissolve to: pan right across typed words: '... of the original ...' Dissolve to: mid shot from behind of a man in a hat. Track left to medium close-up. Dissolve to: type on paper. Pan right. Dissolve to: a photo, mid shot of Mabo family members holding up banners. Zoom in to close-up of Bonita. Wide shot of a boat on the water. Pan left to mid shot of a man in a boat.

Still more controversial was the Court's decision the principles applied in the Mabo case could establish native title on the mainland, too.

A boat railing moves past the distant island. Fade music.

JEFF KENNETT: As a result of Mabo there will be dozens, if not hundreds, of claims ...

Wide shot of water and boat, the island rising up behind. Zoom out.

TIM FISCHER: [*voice over*] ... It may place in jeopardy so many mining projects ...

FOURTH MALE REPORTER: [*voice over*] A further twenty-five claims could be made under Mabo ...

SECOND FEMALE REPORTER: [*voice over*] An Aboriginal group claimed a Government building in Sydney centre ...

A television with a lamp on it. Another reporter is doing a piece to camera.

Pan left across the room to Netta, knitting.

FIFTH MALE REPORTER: A new era, a milestone ...

TREVOR: [*voice over*] 'Mabo' now stood for a case, a cause, an issue, a problem ... a bone of contention for a nation to chew on.

Television news, a close-up of John Hewson in Parliament. Zoom in.

JOHN HEWSON: This is a day of shame for the Australian Parliament ...

Television news, an extreme close-up of Paul Keating.

PAUL KEATING: ... A day when we recognise that indigenous Australians had a right to their own soil ...

Television news, a close-up of Richard Court. Jump to extreme close-up.

RICHARD COURT: We have eighty percent of Western Australia can be claimed ...

Television, an extreme close-up of Jeff Ewing, with dark hair and beard.

JEFF EWING: Over seventy-five percent of the country ...

Television, an extreme close-up of bespectacled Bill Hassell.

BILL HASSELL: ... Potential to destroy our society ...

Bonita's hands continue knitting.

ROBERT TICKNER: [*voice over*] This is a concerted campaign by the leader of the opposition

Television close-up of Robert Tickner. Zoom in.

[*Sync*] ... To cause fear and loathing, hatred and division ...

Television Medium close-up of John Hewson with his arms folded. Cut to extreme close-up.

JOHN HEWSON: ... All over Australia who are going to be significantly worse off ...

Mid shot of Bonita, still sitting and knitting.

JEFF KENNETT: [*voice over*] We do not recognise native title ...

SIXTH MALE REPORTER: [*voice over*] Mabo and it's implications were ...

BRYAN KEON-COHEN: [*voice over*] Leading politicians made some very extreme and unjustifiable statements which seemed to have no foundation other than to whip up some anti-Mabo frenzy.

A newspaper photo. Dissolve to: the headline: 'Mabo Clash'. Dissolve to: a newspaper photo. Zoom out to an Australia map. Medium close-up of Bryan Keon-Cohen outside the High Court building.

[*Sync*] It's as if the propertied elements of this country believe the· High Court was there to protect their rights and deny anyone else's ability to challenge those rights, even if those rights were founded on a legal fiction called '*terra nullius*'.

A framed photo of three women(?). Tilt down the wall of other photos.

TREVOR: [*out of view*] What do you think about the court case now?

MALITA: [*out of view*] It's gotten too deep for me, it goes too far; it's just a name now, no one behind the name: that's how I think about it.

Close-up of Malita.

TREVOR: [*out of view*] Are you proud of your dad?

MALITA: [*sync*] Yeah, I'm proud of my dad, but as I said, it's just a name; they don't know who the name belongs to, or anything like that, or what he's like.

Black.

Fade up intertitle: 'The Journey Home'.

Wide shot of graves and a hill behind. Super: 'June 1995'. Bird sounds. Medium close-up of Eddie Jnr wiping. Tilt down to the grave stone.

TREVOR: [*voice over*] Islander tradition provided the family with the ideal occasion to remind the world that Eddie Mabo was not a case, but a human being.

Close-up of Bonita in the graveyard.

[*Out of view*] So how long have you been preparing this, Bonita?

BONITA: Months …

MALITA: [*out of view*] Since last year.

TREVOR: [*voice over*] After three years, the period for mourning Eddie's death was over. The time had come to celebrate his life, and his famous victory, and what that meant for all the indigenous people of Australia.

Wide shot of Bonita, Eddie Jnr and Malita at the grave site. Medium close-up of Eddie Mabo Jnr. Tilt down to his hand wiping the headstone.

EDDIE JNR: You recording this? Rat!

Mid shot of Malita walking by the graves.

TREVOR: The simple wooden cross that had marked his grave in Townsville Cemetery was replaced by a marble headstone.

MALITA: You can see that mark when you stand on this side, you can see that ...

EDDIE JNR: [*out of view*] Why we leave the headstone to be unveiled at a later date rather than immediately after a funeral is because there is a grieving period ...

Close-up of Bonita looking at the tombstone. Close-up of Koiki's sculpted face on the headstone. Tilt down to the engraved words.

Well, it's been three years now since Dad died, and tomorrow is going to be June the Third, the anniversary of the High Court decision.

Medium-wide shot of the family grouped around the grave posing for a photograph.

TREVOR: [*out of view*] Eddie, come out a bit more ...

Close-up of Trevor taking a snapshot.

[*Voice over*] It was Netta's idea to ask me to film the unveiling of Eddie's headstone.

A black-and-white photo, mid shot of the group around the headstone. Medium close-up of Eddie Jnr.

EDDIE JNR: We've got a special thing here because of the headstone as it is, I didn't want to show anyone, really. It was going to be a surprise, so what we're doing is wrapping the headstone and then, I think later on today, some of Dad's sisters will come out and add more to it.

Mid shot of Bonita and Malita with red cloth. Close-up Bonita with glasses, a pin in her mouth. Medium-wide shot of Bonita and Malita, red cloth and graves. Close-up of Bonita looking left. Extreme close-up of a finger pushing a pin into the cloth. Baskets. Zoom out to medium-wide shot of women and baskets. Close-up of a man in glasses and cap. Tilt down to a bamboo pole.

We build a small fence around the grave site and that will be decorated with bananas, yams, leaves and such.

Medium close-up of a man in a light blue shirt, talking. Baskets and jewellery. Zoom out to medium-wide shot of the decorated grave. Medium-wide shot of gravestones.

THIRD FEMALE REPORTER: [*voice over*] And you described it earlier as a celebration: is it not a sombre event?

Medium-wide shot of seated women and bowls of food. Music and singing.

EDDIE JNR: [*voice over*] With our tradition, going into a death, you are moving into another life, you're moving into a better place, the after life. You understand what I'm saying?

Hands slice sweet potato into a bowl. Other hands slice yams into a bowl. A knife slices food. Medium-wide shot of a group at the bench preparing the food. Hands and sponges. Zoom out to mid shot of a woman.

THIRD FEMALE REPORTER: [*voice over*] Yes, so this is a celebration of your father moving into a better life.
EDDIE JNR: [*voice over*] Yes.

Medium-wide shot of a child dancing. Medium-wide shot of kids and a woman at a table, clapping. Medium-wide shot of a group of men preparing food in the open. Fade out music and singing.

THIRD FEMALE REPORTER: [*voice over*] Now, Eddie, Townsville is obviously a long way from Murray Island; how many people from Murray Island and indeed other Torres Strait islands are coming for the weekend?

Close-up food wrapped in leaves over coals. Tilt up to mid shot of two men. Close-up of Eddie Jnr with a mobile phone to his ear.

EDDIE JNR: Well, I don't think there's too many people left on Murray Island at this point of time.
THIRD FEMALE REPORTER: [*voice over*] So there's a lot of them about?

Medium-wide shot of a crowd of people outside. Two women shake hands.

EDDIE JNR: [*voice over*] Yes, and I'm really thankful that Mrs Keating could make it and also Mr and Mrs Tickner.

Close-up of Anita Keating, smiling. Pan right to Netta, also smiling. Close-up of Eddie Jnr on the mobile phone.

[*Sync*] You know, the way I see it is, this is just the wider Australian community paying respects for my father and I'm thankful for that.

It's just amazing.

A wide shot of marchers with grass skirts on a road in the heart of Townsville. Drumming.

THIRD FEMALE REPORTER: [*voice over*] Eddie Koiki Mabo was a crusader. Today indigenous people have marched united in his name on the third anniversary of the land-rights High Court decision

Close-up of a T-shirt: 'I'm proud of you Darling'. Tilt up to close-up of Bonita. Close-up of a T-shirt with a picture of Koiki on it. Tilt up to the many faces of the marchers..

LOIS O'DONOGHUE: [*voice over*] We indigenous Australians always knew that Terra Nullius was wrong but, until nineteen ninety-two, Australian law did not recognise our title to our land.

Close-up of a child with a Torres Strait flag. Medium-wide shot of people walking with Torres Strait and Aboriginal flags. Wide shot from above the marching crowd. Fade out drumming. Close-up of Lois O'Donoghue at a microphone. Super: 'LOIS O'DONOGHUE, Chairperson ATSIC, 1990-1995'.

[*Sync*] The High Court decision changed this and it changed Australia forever.

Medium-wide shot of the crowd approaching, Bonita centre. Zoom in to mid shot of Anita Keating.

[*Voice over*] Today we are celebrating the life and the struggle of Eddie Mabo. For Aboriginal and Torres Strait Islander people, he is a hero.

Medium-wide shot of the crowd gathered in the Townsville Cemetery. Anita Keating and Bonita move into position. Close-up of people singing. Wide shot of many people. Close-up of Donald Whaleboat in a white T-shirt speaking in the crowd. Fade out singing.

DONALD WHALEBOAT: This is the official end of mourning when sorry is finished. This is time when we will rejoice that we know that his spirit is resting in peace, but his spirit is also still here with us though.

Medium close-up of Anita Keating and Bonita at the graveside. Close-up of Bryan Keon-Cohen in a cap taking a snapshot. Close-up of Eddie Mabo

Jnr. Medium close-up of two women in white tops, one taping the speech. Medium-wide shot of a crowd of people behind headstones.

When this unveiling of the tombstone takes place that also means that the partner is also free.

Close-up Bonita's head bowed. Mid shot of faces in the crowd. Women with colourful headbands cut the ribbon to the gravesite. Zoom out to the crowd. Pan left to the grave.

We are happy that what Koiki has done for us and also we are happy that he also has a place to rest.

Music and singing. Close-up of a woman in song. Medium-wide shot of Bonita moving through the crowd, Anita Keating following. Pan left, following the action, to the grave.

TREVOR: [*voice over*] It seemed to me, as we filmed, that all the conflicting strands of Koiki's fractious life were being pulled together. And reconciliation seemed a real possibility that day.

Singing faces in the crowd. Pan right.

There was another reconciliation too - with the island community he'd quarrelled with and fought for all his life.

Medium-wide shot of men folding cloth. Zoom in to mid two-shot. Medium close-up of Bonita crying. Close-up of a woman, face half hidden behind white cloth. Mid shot of men drawing away cloth from the grave. Close-up of Anita Keating. Close-up of a woman with a hand to her face. Pink cloth is drawn away to reveal the headstone. Zoom in to Koiki's portrait in bass relief. Close-up of Bonita bowing her head. Zoom out to include other faces. Close-up five shot. Close-up of a boy with a tear on his face. The headstone, reflecting the mourners. Fade out music and singing. Wide shot of the cemetery at dusk. Music and singing. A dancer's headdress. Tilt down the dancer's body to his feet.

TREVOR: That night the Murray Islanders danced to celebrate the life of Eddie Koiki Mabo.

Wide shot of dancers in pink costumes. Track left to mid shot of Bonita. Mid shot of a little girl dancing with a grass skirt. Close-up of the dancers' feet. Medium close-up of a male dancer with a pink headband. Long shot of a row of dancers in pink. Close-up of two women's faces. Wide shot of dancers in grass skirts and tall headdresses. Wide shot of two dancers in yellow and blue skirts. Wide aerial shot of Townsville at night. Pan right and zoom out to extreme wide shot of the city. Fade to black. Fade out music and singing.

Fade up intertitle: 'The next morning'.

Fade to black. Fade up wide shot of a police car in front of the cemetery. Red spray paint on the headstone spells: 'ABO'. Zoom out to a mid shot of a man cleaning the painted letters off the headstone. Pan left to medium close-up of a distraught Netta. Close-up of a painted red swastika. Close-up of Bonita wiping tears away. Close-up of a woman with her hair in a bun. Medium close-up of men approaching. The headstone, daubed with red paint. Tilt down to the red swastika above the engraved words. Mid shot of the grouped relatives comforting each other. Bonita cries. Wide shot of people and a cameraman around the grave. Mid shot of a man and woman in red and yellow.

MAN: This is very sad.

CELUIA: [*sync*] It sucks really.

Hands point to cracks and damage in the headstone where the image of Koiki used to be.

MAN: He'd been cut, he got something left inside. But there's none left, there's only hole there.

The base of the painted headstone.

CHILD: [*out of view*] 'Abo'.

Medium-wide shot of Margaret Reynolds with two of Koiki's grandchildren pointing to the grave.

[*Sync*] What does 'Abo' mean?

MARGARET REYNOLDS: It doesn't really mean anything; it's a bad word.

Medium close-up of Margaret Reynolds with the grave site behind her.

It's a very sad day for Australia, I think,when a national hero for the indigenous community and indeed for many fair minded Australians would ... we would see this desecration.

Mid shot of Bonita and three grandchildren sitting by the grave. The sound of crying, camera flashes. Close-up child in tears. Tilt up to close-up of Bonita. Close-up of a child with a tear dropping down his cheek. Close-up of

Bonita's head bowed close to the child's. Her big hand covers his little one. Close-up of Bonita, sombre. Pan right to a female reporter. Zoom out to a mid shot of Bonita facing the microphone.

FOURTH FEMALE REPORTER: [*out of view*] Okay, and the grave looked so lovely yesterday, and now this today; how does it make you feel?

BONITA: Sick to the stomach. It went over so beautiful yesterday and to wake up to this, it's a nightmare starting all over again.

Medium-wide shot of television reporters and Bonita.

FOURTH FEMALE REPORTER: How would you describe the people who are responsible for this?

Close-up of Bonita.

BONITA: They are just a low down mob of racist bastards.

A television screen: extreme close-up of a man's face. Zoom out a little to reveal a senior police officer.

POLICEMAN: It could be white adults involved, it could be Aboriginal or Islander juveniles involved.

Extreme close-up.

It is purely and simply an investigation of a wilful damage at this stage as far as the Queensland police service is concerned.

Close-up of a man's head bowed by the headstone.

FIFTH FEMALE REPORTER: [*voice over*] There was supposed to be no more tears after yesterday's tombstone opening. In the spirit of Islander culture there was only to be dancing and the whole country was welcomed. This is how that trust was repaid.

Medium close-up of men gathered around the headstone. Close-up of the men's faces bowed. Close-up of Danny West looking at the headstone. Medium-wide shot looking up from ground people lifting headstone. Medium-wide shot putting headstone on truck. Mid shot of Danny, sombre. The headstone is loaded on a truck. Close-up of Eddie Jnr looking through the white-grilled side of the tray. Tilt down to the headstone as the truck drives off. Pan right to follow the action into wide shot.

EDDIE JNR: [*voice over*] We had a family meeting and it was unanimous that we exhume Dad's body and we take him back to a peaceful resting place at Las. That was his wish initially.

Mid shot of Eddie Jnr sitting at grave site.

[*Sync*] So I don't see that we've got a lot of choice; we've got to take him back. And you see, what was supposed to be the end of mourning is now just ... all the wounds are opened up again. It's like we've got to go through this further.

Close-up of Gail, crying.

GAIL: I said, 'I don't want to take my dad away. I want to leave him in Townsville'. But I thought, 'No, I'm outvoted. Everybody wants to take him to Murray, so I'll have to go with it'. I thought, 'Where am I going to get the money to go to Murray Island? I can't'.

Wide shot of the sun's rays over the graves in Townsville Cemetery. Pan left.

[*Voice* over] I thought, 'How am I going to put flowers on his grave?'

Medium-wide shot of a man digging Koiki's gravesite, flowers in the foreground. Medium-wide shot from in front of the man. A shovel pries the plaque off Koiki's coffin. The plaque reads: 'Edward Mabo, Aged 55 years'. Fade to black. Music.

Fade up extreme wide aerial shot over Murray Island. Extreme wide aerial shot of two islands. Wide shot of a plane in the sky. Tilt down as it lands in a field. Pan left with the action to a wide shot of a group. Fade music. Close-up of Netta in flower hat looking left. Wide shot from behind two men in grass skirts looking at the plane. Mid shot of people looking right. Zoom out to medium-wide shot. Medium-wide shot from behind four men carrying the coffin. Track with them to the crowd in the distance. The sound of wailing. Close-up of Bonita, also in a hat, crying. Zoom out as the coffin passes. Wide shot of the funeral procession approaching on foot. Mid shot of two women walking right with others. Mid shot of the coffin passing left to right. Medium close-up of Bonita from behind. Track with her through the bush. Wide shot from the water of the land. Pan right. Dissolve to: medium-wide shot of the bamboo wall and trees on the beach. Pan right.

EDDIE JNR: [*voice over*] Well, the ten-year battle of the land claim was for this place, it was for this.

Dissolve to: mid shot of Eddie Jnr.

[*Sync*] Now, the significance of the place where we're going to bury him is that his ancestors are not far from his final resting place.

Music and singing. Mid shot of traditionally dressed pallbearers approaching with the coffin. Long shot of the funeral procession approaching through the bush. Wide shot of the head of the procession, a photographer screen right. Medium-wide shot of pallbearers setting down the coffin. Close up of two relatives, heads together, crying. Tilt down to close-up of a grandchild. Medium-wide shot of tearful faces crying, looking to the right.

TREVOR: [*voice over*] Amongst the islanders who came to pay their last respects, there was a strong sense that this was where Koiki really belonged.

Long shot of pallbearers setting down the coffin, mourners in background. Medium close-up of Jack Wailu and a child.

JACK WAILU: [*subtitled*] I used to think, 'One day I will see Eddie, one day I will see Eddie, Eddie must return home'. I had a strong feeling that Eddie must return home.

Medium close-up of the bare backs of pallbearers lowering the coffin, mourners in the distance. Close-up of two people crying. High angle shot of the coffin lid. Medium close-up of Bonita holding a grandchild.

TREVOR: [*voice over*] I found I had mixed feelings. There was a sense of rightness about Koiki coming home to Mer. But his family had had to bring him here for all the wrong reasons.

The plaque on the coffin, a little sand on it. Tilt up to a cross. Zoom out to a wider shot of the coffin in the grave.

I remembered him saying he hoped the Mabo case would help unite Australia, and not divide it.

Fade out music and singing. Mid shot of Bonita in a hat, standing by the headstone. Pan right to a medium-wide shot of mourners. Pan left back to Bonita.

I felt ashamed that Netta and her family had been forced to make this choice, just to keep him safe.

Wide shot, the headstone in foreground, of mourners and a photographer. Close-up of Bonita looking left. Tilt down to the headstone and a new bass-relief portrait of Koiki.

BONITA: [*voice over*] The hardest part is for me now to … to go back to Townsville and sort of leave him up here …

Mid shot of Bonita speaking in front of the grave.

[*Sync*] … But then again I suppose I'd have to let go. I've got no choice, do I ? But anyhow … But I do feel a lot more at ease now to know that he's here, yeah.

Wide shot of a seagull in the sky. Tilt down as it dives into the water, fishing. Music and singing. Wide shot of the shore at dusk, two people fishing. Pan left to the bamboo wall on the sand. Wide shot looking out to sea through a gap in the bamboo wall. Wide shot silhouette of palm trees against a pink sky. Wide shot by moonlight looking out to sea through a gap in the bamboo wall. Close-up of Jack Wailu, back lit, looking screen left. Wide shot silhouette of dancers watched by a circle of people. Close-up of a dancer in a Malo mask. Zoom out to whole long shot. Medium close-up of Bonita holding a sleeping child. Close-up of the child's face, looking right. Close-up of an old man looking left. Mid shot of a dancer with a big Malo mask.

TREVOR: [*voice over*] That night, the islanders performed the sacred Malo dance, in honour of Koiki Mabo, the man who'd won them recognition of their land, and law, and custom.

Mid shot of the backs of dancers at night. Medium close-up of a child's face looking right, by lamplight. An old hand on a drum. Tilt up to Jack Wailu's face. Mid shot of the dancers in the dark. Tilt down to other dancers lying on the ground.

In daylight, legs wade into water. Tilt up to mid shot of Koiki with a spear. Close-up of James Rice in cap and glasses.

JAMES RICE: I really appreciate that Koiki came back again to his native land. He is buried in his own land. I really appreciated him to settle down at Las.

Medium-wide shot back of Koiki with spear, walking in water.

Late, Eddie Koiki Mabo.

Wide shot of water and horizon, Koiki with his spear. Fade to black. Fade up title, 'In Memory of JACK WAILU, 1936-1996'. Roll credits.

Film Credits

This film was made between 1989 and 1997 by Director & Co-producer TREVOR GRAHAM/Producer and Editor DENISE HASLEM/Executive Producer SHARON CONNOLLY/Cinematographer JOHN WHITTERON/Sound Recordist & Designer BRONWYN MURPHY/In association with the MABO FAMILY and THE PEOPLE OF MURRAY ISLAND/Participants BONITA MABO, EDDIE MABO JNR, GAIL MABO, MARIO MABO, CELUIA MABO, MALITA WEST, DANNY WEST, BRYAN KEON-COHEN/NOEL LOOS, HENRY REYNOLDS, MARGARET REYNOLDS, DONALD WHALEBOAT, FATHER DAVE PASSI, JACK WAILU, JAMES RICE, PAUL SMITH, ERIC WILLMOT/Land Bilong Islanders Participants JUSTICE MARTIN MOYNIHAN, MARWAR DIPOMA, KABA NOAH, EDDIE KOIKI MABO.

Narration Writer JONATHAN HOLMES/Music composers DAVID BRIDIE, JOHN PHILLIPS/Sound Mixer PETER WALKER/ Additional Eddie Voice BOB MAZA/Production Manager NICKY McGINN/Production Supervisors IAN ADKINS, FRANK HAINES/Promotions Manager MICHELLE O'RIORDAN/Camera Assistants GRANT CAWOOD, JAMES BURKE/Editing Assistant FELICITY NEALE/Production Accountants JANETTE GOULD, CAROLYN JOHNSON/Production Assistants JEANNINE BAKER, JANE MANNING, JULIE ADAMS/TEAME Trainee SARAH MASON/ Sound Mix Facilities SOUNDWAVES/Additional Cinematography BRUCE BLACK/Archival Stills Photography SANDRA IRVINE/ Additional Musicians DAVID ABUISO, CHRIS WILSON, GULUPA GOLKAMA, KEREKA KAU/Sound Transfers SOUNDFIRM/ Optical FX BRUCE BLAKE, ACME DIGITAL/Titles OPTICAL & GRAPHIC/Post-Production Facilities FILM AUSTRALIA/Neg Matching CHRIS ROWELL/Laboratory MOVIELAB/Grader KELVIN CRUMPLIN/Kines DFILM SERVICES/Telecine FRAME SET & MATCH/Colorist PETER

SIMPSON/Transcripts CLEVER TYPES/Subtitles SPEAKING IN TONGUES/Produced with the assistance of THE AUSTRALIAN BROADCASTING CORPORATION/ABC Executive Producer DASHA ROSS.

Archives BONITA MABO COLLECTION, YARRA BANK FILMS PTY LTD, AIATSIS SPECIAL COLLECTIONS, AIATSIS PHOTO LIBRARY, NATIONAL LIBRARY OF AUSTRALIA, NATIONAL LIBRARY MABO PAPERS, NATIONAL LIBRARY ORAL COLLECTION, QUEENSLAND RAILWAYS HISTORICAL COLLECTION, JAMES COOK UNIVERSITY ARCHIVES, JOHN OXLEY LIBRARY/JOAN MILES, NOEL LOOS, MAUREEN FUARY, TREVOR GRAHAM, SEARCH FOUNDATION, CHANNEL 10 TOWNSVILLE, NATIONAL FILM AND SOUND ARCHIVE, FILM AUSTRALIA, ABC FOOTAGE LIBRARY, ABC RADIO ARCHIVES, DAVID BILCOCK SNR, AUSTRALIAN BAR ASSOCIATION, PRISM PRODUCTIONS, MARITIME UNION OF AUSTRALIA.

The producers wish to thank THE PEOPLE OF MURRAY ISLAND, JEREMY BECKETT, NOEL LOOS, BRUCE MOIR, NONI SHARP and MEB and ADDEE SALEE, BRETT and RITA TYRELL, GEORGE KUDUB, JACKSON WAILU, SAM WAILU, BAI DAY, RON DAY, FATHER GIZU, HENRY KABERE, MARINDA KOIKI, JOHN KOIKI, CHARLES PASSI, NICEY SAMBO, WILFRED TAPAU/MARTHA ANSARA, KIRSTY ALFREDSON, ZITA ANTONIUS, KIM BATTERHAM, JUDY BELL, KARIN CALLEY, DEBORAH CASS, RON CASTAN, LARRY CROMWELL, JUNE EDWARDS, JOHN FLETCHER, FINA FICHURA, PAT FISKE, WAYNE HAYES, PAT KENNEDY, BARBARA HOCKING, ANDREW LAWRENCE, BILL JONAS, IAN KENTWELL/NED LANDER, DAVE LANE, SIR ANTHONY MASON, GREG McINTYRE, JOAN MILES, CRAIG MUNRO, NOEL PEARSON, GRAHAM POWELL, LIBBY PRICE, ZOE REYNOLDS, CHRIS ROWELL, KEN SALLOWS, RON STORE, GLENN SCHWINGHAMMER, ROBERT TICKNER, FRED THOMPSON, MARGARET WHITE, GAYE WOODS, RAY VALDETTA/HIGH COURT OF AUSTRALIA, SUPREME COURT OF QUEENSLAND, QUEENSLAND DEPARTMENT OF CROWN LAW, QUEENSLAND POLICE SERVICE –

TOWNSVILLE, JAMES COOK UNIVERSITY, STATE LIBRARY OF NSW, ROYAL NORTH SHORE HOSPITAL/TOWNSVILLE GENERAL HOSPITAL, BELGIAN GARDEN CEMETERY, MAWLEY'S FUNERAL SERVICE, HUMAN RIGHTS AND EQUAL OPPORTUNITY COMMISSION, MELVILLE HIGH SCHOOL, SOUTH KEMPSEY PRIMARY SCHOOL, TELSTRA HISTORICAL ARTIFACTS.

Additional Music 'Traditional Music of the Torres Strait' by JEREMY BECKETT, AUSTRALIAN INSTITUTE OF ABORIGINAL AND TORRES STRAIT ISLANDER STUDIES/'Baba Wain', 'Taba Naba' THE MILLS SISTERS, FRANGIPANI LAND/'Kape Ka Tebteb', 'Sunbird Ide' TORRES STRAIT ISLANDS MEDIA ASSOCIATION /'Land Bilong Islanders' composed by KOIKI MABO and JACK WAILU

A FILM AUSTRALIA NATIONAL INTEREST PROGRAM.

SCREENPLAYS FROM CURRENCY PRESS

Strictly Ballroom
Baz Luhrmann and Craig Pearce

The Adventures of Priscilla, Queen of the Desert
Stephan Elliott

Muriel's Wedding
P.J. Hogan

The Sum of Us
David Stevens

Bad Boy Bubby
Rolf de Heer

Cosi
Louis Nowra

Dead Heart
Nick Parsons

Children of the Revolution
Peter Duncan

Love Serenade
Shirley Barrett

Blackrock
Nick Enright

Scales of Justice
Robert Caswell

Road to Nhill
Alison Tilson

Mabo – Life of an Island Man
Trevor Graham

The Boys
Stephen Sewell

3 Screenplays
Paul Cox

Spotswood
Max Dann and Andrew Knight

Women of the Sun
Hyllus Maris and Sonia Borg

Dingo
Marc Rosenberg

Angel Baby
Michael Rymer

ALL INQUIRIES TO:
Currency Press,
PO Box 2287,
Strawberry Hills,
NSW 2012
Tel: 02 9319 5877
Fax: 02 9319 3649
E-mail: currency@magna.com.au
WWW: http://www.currency.com.au